THANK YOU, AMERICA!

VERONICA BROWN

authorHOUSE™

1663 LIBERTY DRIVE, SUITE 200
BLOOMINGTON, INDIANA 47403
(800) 839-8640
WWW.AUTHORHOUSE.COM

First published by AuthorHouse 11/16/05

ISBN: 1-4208-8537-5 (sc)

Printed in the United States of America
Bloomington, Indiana

This book is printed on acid-free paper.

(KOUMBA DESIGNERS) KOUMBA'S FASHION DESIGNING INSTITUTE, COCOTIER, COTONOU.

KOUMBA: HELLO, MR. MINISTER. HOW IS YOUR FAMILY?

MR. MINISTER: VERY WELL; I THANK YOU. HAVE YOU BEEN ABLE TO FINISH WITH MY WIFE'S CLOTHES?

KOUMBA: NO, I HAVE HAD TOO MUCH WORK, BUT YOU SAID HER BIRTHDAY IS NEXT WEEK?

MR. MINISTER: YES, IT IS. I WOULD LIKE TO PRESENT HER WITH THE BOO-BOO AND A PORSCHE. BUT I TRUST YOU WILL GET THE BOO-BOO READY BEFORE NEXT WEEK THURSDAY.

KOUMBA: ABSOLUTELY. I WILL HAVE IT DELIVERED TO HER BY OUR SPECIAL BIRTHDAY DELIVERY SERVICE.

MR. MINISTER: DO YOU WANT ME TO PAY YOU NOW?

KOUMBA: NOT NECESSARILY, MR. MINISTER, UNLESS YOU WISH TO DO SO.

MR. MINISTER: YES, LET ME PAY YOU NOW. HOW MUCH IS IT?

KOUMBA: 200.000 CF, MR. MINISTER.

MR. MINISTER: HERE YOU GO.

KOUMBA: THANK YOU, MR. MINISTER. (KOUMBA COUNTS.) BUT YOU GAVE ME 300.000 CF. IT IS 200.000 CF.

MR. MINISTER: I KNOW. THE 100.000 CF IS FOR THE QUALITY OF YOUR WORK.

KOUMBA: (LAUGHS) THANK YOU, MR. MINISTER. YOU WILL LOVE THE DESIGN.

MR. MINISTER: I KNOW, MISS KOUMBA. I HAVE TO GO NOW. YOU HAVE A LOVELY DAY.

KOUMBA: YOU TOO, MR. MINISTER. HAVE A GREAT DAY.

(THE PHONE RINGS.)

SECRETARY: KOUMBA DESIGNERS. MAY I HELP YOU?

THE FIRST LADY: (ON THE OTHER LINE) YES, IS MISS KOUMBA THERE?

SECRETARY: YES, SHE IS. WHO IS CALLING?

THE FIRST LADY: IT IS THE FIRST LADY, MRS. DIANE.

SECRETARY: GOOD MORNING, MRS. PRESI-DENT. PLEASE HOLD WHILE I CONNECT YOU. *(SHE CONNECTS MISS KOUMBA.)* MISS KOUMBA, THE FIRST LADY IS ON THE LINE FOR YOU.

KOUMBA: OKAY, PASS HER ON. MRS. PRESI-DENT, HOW ARE YOU DOING?

THE FIRST LADY: I AM PRETTY FINE, THANK YOU, AND HOW HAVE YOU BEEN?

KOUMBA: PRETTY WELL, THANK YOU. YOUR CLOTHES ARE READY AND ARE GOING TO BE DELIVERED TO YOUR RESIDENCE TODAY.

THE FIRST LADY: GREAT! I WAS CALLING BECAUSE I NEED ONE OF THEM TODAY, FOR A RECEPTION. I HAVE OTHER BOO-BOOS TO SEW. DO YOU THINK YOU COULD STOP BY TOMORROW?

KOUMBA: NO PROBLEM. I WILL SEE YOU TOMORROW.

THE FIRST LADY: HAVE A NICE DAY.

KOUMBA: YOU TOO, MRS. PRESIDENT. HAVE AN EXCELLENT DAY.

(KOUMBA CALLS THE DELIVERY SERVICES TO CHECK WITH THE DAY'S DELIVERIES.)

KOUMBA: MAKE SURE YOU DELIVER THE FIRST LADY'S CLOTHES FIRST BEFORE OTHER DELIVERIES TODAY.

THE ASSISTANT: YES, MISS KOUMBA.

KOUMBA: OKAY, THANK YOU.

THE ASSISTANT: THANK YOU, MISS KOUMBA.

(THE PHONE RINGS.)

SECRETARY: KOUMBA DESIGNERS. MAY I HELP YOU?

TOGO'S FIRST LADY: (ON THE OTHER LINE) YES, IS MISS KOUMBA THERE?

SECRETARY: YES, SHE IS. WHO IS CALLING?

TOGO'S FIRST LADY: IT IS TOGO'S FIRST LADY, MRS. KOUAME.

SECRETARY: GOOD MORNING, MRS. KOUAME. PLEASE HOLD WHILE I CONNECT YOU. *(SHE CONNECTS MISS KOUMBA.)* MISS KOUMBA, TOGO'S FIRST LADY, MRS. KOUAME IS ON THE LINE FOR YOU.

KOUMBA: OKAY, PASS HER ON. MRS. PRESIDENT, HOW ARE YOU DOING?

TOGO'S FIRST LADY: FINE, THANK YOU. MY DRIVER IS COMING TO COTONOU TO GIVE YOU TEN MATERIALS TO SEW FOR ME. I ALSO SENT PAGES OF YOUR CATALOGUE WITH THE PRECISE DESIGNS I WOULD LIKE ON EACH BOO-BOO. HE HAS LEFT AND SHOULD BE IN COTONOU IN TWO HOURS' TIME.

KOUMBA: NO PROBLEM. SHOULD I STILL USE THE SAME MEASUREMENTS?

TOGO'S FIRST LADY: YES. I WILL GO AHEAD AND TRANSFER THE TOTAL PRICE INTO YOUR ACCOUNT. THE PRICE IS STILL THE SAME?

KOUMBA: YES, MOSTLY, BUT I WILL HAVE TO SEE THE DESIGNS YOU WANT FIRST. I WILL CALL YOU BACK AS SOON AS YOUR DRIVER GETS HERE. ARE YOU GOING TO BE HOME?

TOGO'S FIRST LADY: I AM LEAVING THE RESIDENCE NOW, BUT I WILL BE BACK HOME BEFORE 6 PM. HOW LATE ARE YOU OPEN?

KOUMBA: WE CLOSE AT 9 PM.

TOGO'S FIRST LADY: OKAY, GREAT. I WILL BE HOME LONG BEFORE YOU CLOSE.

KOUMBA: I WILL CALL YOU THEN, BEFORE I LEAVE.

TOGO'S FIRST LADY: ALL RIGHT. YOU HAVE A NICE DAY.

KOUMBA: YOU TOO, MRS. PRESIDENT.

TOGO'S FIRST LADY: BYE FOR NOW.

KOUMBA: BYE, MRS. PRESIDENT. TALK TO YOU LATER.

KOUMBA GOES ON SEWING THE PRESIDENT'S BOO-BOO HERSELF; SHE DOES NOT WANT ANY OF HER STAFF TO SEW IT.

SHE LOOKS AROUND TO SEE WHAT HER STAFF IS DOING. SHE CORRECTS THEM WHEN NECESSARY AND CREDITS THEM WHEN NECESSARY ...

(THE PHONE RINGS.)

SECRETARY: KOUMBA DESIGNERS. MAY I HELP YOU?

LAURENT: HELLO, IS KOUMBA THERE?

SECRETARY: YES, SHE IS. WHO IS CALLING?

LAURENT: IT'S LAURENT.

SECRETARY: GOOD MORNING, SIR. PLEASE HOLD ON WHILE I CONNECT YOU. *(SHE CONNECTS MISS KOUMBA.)* MISS KOUMBA, MR. LAURENT IS ON THE LINE FOR YOU.

KOUMBA: OKAY, I'LL TAKE HIM IN MY OFFICE. HELLO, LAURENT, HOW ARE YOU DOING TODAY?

LAURENT: I AM FINE. I HAD A WONDERFUL NIGHT LAST NIGHT. THANK YOU SO MUCH.

KOUMBA: I ALSO HAD A BEAUTIFUL NIGHT. YOU KNOW WHAT? MY FAMILY IS WORRIED ABOUT ME ...

LAURENT: WHY ARE THEY WORRIED ABOUT YOU? YOU ARE A SUCCESSFUL FASHION DESIGNER. I SEE NO REASON WHY THEY SHOULD BE ...

KOUMBA: NO, YOU DON'T UNDERSTAND ...

LAURENT: UNDERSTAND WHY THEY ARE WORRIED? ... THERE'S NO—

KOUMBA: NO, YOU DON'T UNDERSTAND. YOU SEE, WE'VE BEEN GOING OUT FOR TWO YEARS, AND WE HAVE NOT EVEN TOLD THEM WE ARE GETTING MARRIED, NEITHER ARE WE PLANNING ON GETTING ENGAGED. I AM GOING TO BE THIRTY-FIVE IN A MONTH, AND I STILL AM NOT SURE IF I HAVE FOUND THE RIGHT MAN OR NOT.

LAURENT: KOUMBA, I REALLY AM NOT YET READY TO SETTLE DOWN. WE STILL HAVE TIME ...

KOUMBA: I THINK WE HAVE TO GET TOGETHER TO TALK ABOUT THIS. WHERE ARE YOU NOW? CAN YOU COME BY HERE?

LAURENT: OKAY, I'LL BE THERE IN THIRTY MINUTES.

KOUMBA: OKAY, SEE YOU LATER.

LAURENT: OKAY, LOVE YOU.

KOUMBA: ME TOO.

KOUMBA GOES OUT OF HER OFFICE AND CONTINUES TO LOOK AT WHAT HER STAFF IS

DOING. SHE SITS DOWN WITH ONE OF THEM TO FINISH UP WHAT SHE HAD STARTED.

SOON LAURENT WALKS IN THE BOUTIQUE, AND KOUMBA GIVES THE JOB BACK TO HER STAFF.

KOUMBA: LAURENT, HOW ARE YOU DOING?

LAURENT: FINE, AND YOU?

KOUMBA: LET'S GO TO MY OFFICE ... (TURNS TO THE SECRETARY) I AM NOT ANSWERING CALLS NOW. TELL WHOEVER CALLS THAT I WILL CALL THEM BACK.

SECRETARY: OKAY, MISS KOUMBA.

LAURENT AND KOUMBA WALK TO KOUMBA'S OFFICE AND SIT DOWN.

LAURENT: THIS PLACE IS SO CUTE ...

KOUMBA: THANK YOU. NOW, WHAT I WAS TELLING YOU ON THE PHONE ...

LAURENT : YES.

KOUMBA: YOU SEE, MY PARENTS ARE REALLY WORRIED. THEY THINK BY THE TIME I GET MARRIED IT MIGHT BE DIFFICULT FOR ME TO HAVE KIDS.

LAURENT: THEY ARE NOT DOCTORS, ARE THEY?

KOUMBA: WHAT DO YOU MEAN THEY ARE NOT DOCTORS? I ALSO NEED TO KNOW WHAT IS HAPPENING IN OUR RELATIONSHIP. DO YOU PLAN ON SOLIDIFYING IT ONE DAY?

LAURENT: I REALLY DO NOT KNOW NOW. LET TOMORROW COME.

KOUMBA: BUT I AM NOT GETTING ANY YOUNGER.

LAURENT: SO, WHAT DO YOU WANT TO DO? I DON'T EVEN THINK I WANT TO GET MAR-RIED, AT LEAST FOR NOW.

KOUMBA: BUT, LAURENT, YOU ARE FORTY-TWO YEARS OLD NOW. I THINK YOU WANT TO KEEP MESSING AROUND. AM I NOT RIGHT?

LAURENT: I DO NOT MESS AROUND AND WOULD NOT ALLOW FOR YOU TO TALK TO ME THAT WAY. I AM A MAN, AND YOU MUST RESPECT ME ACCORDING TO THE AFRICAN CULTURE.

KOUMBA: I THINK YOU SHOULD LEAVE NOW.

LAURENT: WHAT DO YOU MEAN? IF I WALK OUT OF THAT DOOR, THAT WILL BE THE LAST TIME WE SEE EACH OTHER ...

KOUMBA: I THINK MY LIFE IS MUCH BETTER WITHOUT SOMEONE LIKE YOU ... WHO DOES NOT KNOW WHAT HE WANTS FROM LIFE ...

LAURENT: STOP!!! LET'S CALL IT QUITS!

KOUMBA: OKAY.

LAURENT WALKS OUT OF KOUMBA'S OFFICE AND LEAVES. KOUMBA SITS DOWN FOR A WHILE. THEN SHE GETS UP AND GOES OUT FOR LUNCH TO HER PARENTS' HOUSE.

MAMA: KOUMBA, HONEY, HOW ARE YOU DOING?

KOUMBA: FINE, MAMA. I WANT TO TALK WITH YOU.

MAMA: WHAT ABOUT?

KOUMBA: LAURENT AND I JUST BROKE UP. HE SAID HE DOES NOT THINK HE WANTS TO GET MARRIED.

MAMA: WHAT? I FELT BOTH OF YOU WERE GOING TO GET MARRIED ... YOU'VE BEEN GOING OUT FOR THREE YEARS NOW.

KOUMBA: TWO YEARS.

MAMA: IF HE DOES NOT WANT TO GET MAR-
RIED, THEN IT'S BETTER YOU CALL IT QUITS.

KOUMBA: YES, I KNOW. BUT, MAMA, I LOVE
HIM AND HAVE GOTTEN TO KNOW HIM FOR
SO LONG. IT'S TRUE THAT I DIDN'T WANT TO
GET MARRIED BEFORE, BUT NOW I REALLY
WANT TO GET MARRIED TO THE MAN I LOVE
AND START HAVING CHILDREN.

MAMA: I KNOW. I WANT GRANDCHILDREN.
BUT IT'S BETTER TO BREAK UP WITH HIM
NOW THAN IN FIVE YEARS' TIME WHEN YOU
WILL BE FORTY YEARS OLD AND HE COMES
TO TELL YOU HE'S NOT GETTING MARRIED.
DON'T WORRY, GOD WILL CHOOSE FOR YOU.

KOUMBA: AMEN. I AM TIRED OF DATING MAR-
RIED MEN. ALL THEY WANT TO DO IS PLAY
AROUND. WHEN IT IS OVER, THEY GO BACK
TO THEIR WIVES. I AM SICK AND TIRED OF
THAT ...

MAMA: DON'T WORRY, GOD IS GOOD. LET ME
MAKE SOME FOUFOU FOR YOU AND WE'LL
EAT TOGETHER.

KOUMBA: OKAY, MAMA. I'LL MAKE THE
FOUFOU. DO YOU HAVE SOUP AT HOME?

MAMA: YES. I HAVE OKRA SOUP.

KOUMBA GOES INTO THE KITCHEN AND MAKES SOME FOUFOU FOR HER AND HER MAMA.

THEY BOTH EAT, DISCUSSING LAURENT. AFTER THEY HAVE FINISHED EATING, KOUMBA GOES BACK TO HER BOUTIQUE. WHEN HER FATHER COMES HOME, HER MOTHER TELLS HIM ABOUT WHAT THEIR DAUGHTER IS GOING THROUGH.

FATHER: LET'S GO AND TALK TO SHEU. HE ONLY HAS ONE WIFE.

MAMA: OKAY. LET'S SEND FOR HIM.

HER MAMA CALLS TO ONE OF THE CHILDREN PLAYING IN THE YARD AND ASKS HIM TO GO AND CALL SHEU FROM NEXT DOOR.

FATHER: WHEN HE COMES, LET ME TABLE IT DOWN FOR HIM.

MAMA: OKAY.

SHEU: GOOD AFTERNOON, MAMA, PAPA.

MAMA/FATHER: GOOD AFTERNOON, MY SON. HOW ARE YOU DOING? YOU DIDN'T GO TO WORK?

SHEU: NO, I CAME HOME FOR LUNCH.

MAMA: HOW IS YOUR WIFE AND CHILDREN?

SHEU: FINE. THEY HAVE GONE TO SEE MY MOTHER IN THE VILLAGE AND WILL BE BACK NEXT WEEK.

FATHER: YES, THERE IS SOMETHING I HAVE TO TALK TO YOU ABOUT.

SHEU: YES, PAPA.

FATHER: YOU KNOW MY DAUGHTER, KOUMBA?

SHEU: YES, PAPA, I KNOW HER VERY WELL. WHAT HAPPENED? IS SHE OKAY?

FATHER: OH! *(LAUGHS)* YES, SHE'S OKAY. YOU KNOW HOW SUCCESSFUL SHE IS IN THIS TOWN AND ALL OVER OTHER REGIONS OF OUR WEST AFRICA?

SHEU: ABSOLUTELY, PAPA.

FATHER: THERE IS ONLY ONE THING THAT MAKES ME AND HER MOTHER SAD.

SHEU: WHAT, PAPA?

FATHER: THAT'S A GOOD QUESTION, MY SON. YOU SEE, SHE'S THIRTY-FOUR GOING ON THIRTY-FIVE. SHE DOESN'T EVEN HAVE A CHILD. SHE DOESN'T EVEN HAVE A FIANCÉ. THAT IS WHY WE SENT FOR YOU, MY SON.

SHEU: AH! PAPA. YOU WANT ME TO HELP HER LOOK FOR A HUSBAND?

FATHER: NO! WE WANT YOU TO TAKE HER AS YOUR WIFE. SHE IS RICH AND DOES NOT NEED YOUR MONEY. YOU KNOW THAT?

SHEU: PAPA AND MAMA, IT IS TRUE THAT MY WIFE AND I QUARREL EVERY ONCE IN A WHILE. IT IS ALSO TRUE THAT WE HAVE COME TO YOU TO HELP US RESOLVE OUR DIFFER-ENCES, BUT THAT DOES NOT MEAN I WANT TO LEAVE HER.

FATHER: I KNOW, BUT YOU CAN TAKE MY DAUGHTER AS YOUR SECOND WIFE ...

SHEU: I AM SORRY, PAPA, MAMA ...

FATHER: DON'T SAY ANYTHING NOW; JUST GO AND THINK ABOUT IT.

SHEU: THANK YOU, PAPA ... THERE'S REALLY NOTHING TO THINK ABOUT. I LOVE MY WIFE SO MUCH. AND BESIDES, I LIVED IN A POLYGA-MOUS HOME GROWING UP AND WILL NEVER

PUT MY CHILDREN THROUGH WHAT I WENT THROUGH.

MAMA: SHEU, MY SON. GOD BLESS YOU!

SHEU: AMEN, MAMA.

MAMA: YOU SEE, WHAT PAPA IS SAYING IS FOR YOUR OWN PROGRESS. OUR DAUGHTER IS NOT GOING TO BE A BURDEN TO YOU. SHE WILL HELP YOU AND YOUR WIFE AND CHILDREN ...

SHEU: NO, MAMA. I CAN HELP HER LOOK FOR A MAN. BUT THAT MAN IS DEFINITELY NOT GOING TO BE ME.

FATHER: SHEU, MY SON, I KNOW IT IS SCARY TO GO INTO POLYGAMY. EVEN I MYSELF WENT THROUGH IT BEFORE MY FIRST, SECOND, AND THIRD WIVES DIED. THIS IS WHY MAMA IS THE ONLY WIFE I HAVE SINCE TEN YEARS AGO.

SHEU: OKAY, PAPA. I THANK YOU SO MUCH FOR THE OFFER, BUT THE ANSWER IS NO. I NEED TO GO BACK TO WORK NOW.

PAPA: OKAY, BYE. THANK YOU FOR COMING.

MAMA: BYE!

SHEU: BYE, MAMA AND PAPA. HAVE A GREAT DAY.

("THEY ARE CRAZY. HIS THREE WIVES DIED AND TWENTY OF HIS KIDS DIED. HE WANTS ME TO GO THROUGH THE SAME THING?" HE LAUGHS.)

PAPA: THAT BOY IS VERY STUPID! HOW CAN WE TALK TO HIM IN OUR OLD AGE, AND HE REFUSES TO LISTEN?

MAMA: HE DOES NOT EVEN HAVE ANYTHING. HIS BEETLE CAR IS A WRECK. HE PUSHES IT EVERY MORNING TO GET IT STARTED.

PAPA: I WILL SEND FOR THE BANKER, ADAMU.

MAMA: OH YES! WHY DIDN'T WE THINK OF HIM BEFORE? HE ALREADY HAS THREE WIVES AND WILL BE MORE THAN HAPPY TO TAKE KOUMBA AS HIS FOURTH WIFE.

PAPA: TIDJANI!

TIDJANI: YES, PAPA.

PAPA: STOP PLAYING. GO TO THE BANK IN FRONT THERE, ASK FOR MR. ADAMU, AND TELL HIM PAPA KOUMBA WANTS TO SEE HIM.

TIDJANI: YES, PAPA.

(PAPA AND MAMA ARE TALKING ABOUT HOW THEY ARE GOING TO APPROACH ADAMU WHEN HE WALKS IN, IN THE MIDDLE OF THEIR DISCUSSION.)

ADAMU: PAPA, MAMA, GOOD AFTERNOON.

PAPA: GOOD AFTERNOON, MY SON.

MAMA: GOOD AFTERNOON, MY SON. HOW ARE YOU DOING?

ADAMU: FINE, THANK YOU. THE LITTLE BOY SAID YOU WANT TO SEE ME.

PAPA: YES, MY SON. HOW ARE YOU? PLEASE SIT DOWN.

(ADAMU SITS DOWN.)

PAPA: MY SON, YOU KNOW MY DAUGHTER KOUMBA?

ADAMU: YES, PAPA. I KNOW HER, BUT I HAVE NOT HAD AN OPPORTUNITY TO MEET HER SINCE SHE BECAME THE FAMOUS DESIGNER ...

(LAUGHS! LAUGHS! LAUGHS!)

PAPA: OH! YES! SHE IS FAMOUS.

(LAUGHS! LAUGHS! LAUGHS!)

PAPA: WE HAVE ASKED YOU TO COME HERE BECAUSE WE WOULD LIKE TO GIVE YOU OUR DAUGHTER.

ADAMU: GIVE HER TO ME???

PAPA: YES. WE WANT YOU TO MARRY HER.

(LAUGHS! LAUGHS! LAUGHS!)

ADAMU: IS SHE AWARE OF THIS ARRANGE-MENT?

PAPA: YES, SHE IS.

ADAMU: DOES SHE KNOW ME? HAS SHE ACCEPTED TO BE MY WIFE?

PAPA/MAMA: OF COURSE. SHE HAS.

(LAUGHS! LAUGHS! LAUGHS!)

ADAMU: I WILL BE HONORED TO HAVE HER AS MY WIFE.

(LAUGHS! LAUGHS! LAUGHS!)

PAPA: MY SON. YOU WILL COME HERE TOMOR-ROW AT 11 AM TO MEET MY DAUGHTER.

ADAMU: OKAY, PAPA. I WILL BE HERE.

(LAUGHS! LAUGHS! LAUGHS!)

PAPA: I KNOW YOU ARE WORKING, AND I KNOW YOU WANT TO START GOING BACK TO WORK NOW ...

ADAMU: YES, PAPA.

PAPA: YOU HAVE A NICE DAY NOW. WE'LL SEE YOU TOMORROW AT 11 AM.

ADAMU: OKAY, PAPA. SEE YOU TOMORROW.

PAPA/MAMA: SEE YOU TOMORROW, MY SON.

(ADAMU LEAVES. PAPA AND MAMA GO TO SEE KOUMBA AT HER BOUTIQUE. AS THEY WALK IN, KOUMBA IS FRIGHTENED, BECAUSE SHE IS NOT EXPECTING THEM.)

KOUMBA: PAPA, MAMA, WHAT'S WRONG?

PAPA/MAMA: NOTHING, MY CHILD. NOTHING.

PAPA: WE HAVE COME TO TALK TO YOU ABOUT SOMETHING VERY IMPORTANT.

KOUMBA: LET'S GO TO MY OFFICE.

(THEY GO INTO KOUMBA'S OFFICE AND SIT DOWN.)

KOUMBA: WOULD YOU LIKE SOMETHING TO DRINK?

PAPA: NO, MY DAUGHTER.

MAMA: NO, MY DAUGHTER.

PAPA: KOUMBA, I AM YOUR FATHER, AND I WANT WHAT IS BEST FOR YOU. YOU KNOW THAT?

KOUMBA: YES, PAPA.

PAPA: THIS AFTERNOON, ADAMU THE BANKER ... YOU KNOW ADAMU THE BANKER, DON'T YOU?

KOUMBA: YES. THE ONE THAT WORKS IN THE BANK IN FRONT OF THE HOUSE?

(LAUGHS! LAUGHS! LAUGHS!)

PAPA: YES, MY CHILD. THAT'S IT.

KOUMBA: WHAT HAPPENED TO HIM?

PAPA: NOTHING. IT IS WELL! ADAMU CAME AND ASKED US FOR YOUR HAND IN MAR-RIAGE, AND WE ACCEPTED.

KOUMBA: WHAT? I DON'T EVEN KNOW HIM ... HE IS MARRIED! HE'S BEEN MARRIED WITH TWO WIVES SINCE I WAS IN HIGH SCHOOL!

PAPA: I KNOW, MY DAUGHTER. HE NOW HAS THREE WIVES. HE IS FERTILE! HE HAS FIFTEEN KIDS.

KOUMBA: FIFTEEN KIDS! OH, MY GOD!

PAPA: WHAT WE ARE FIGHTING FOR IS FOR YOU TO GET MARRIED AND HAVE CHILDREN.

KOUMBA: I UNDERSTAND, BUT THAT'S NOT THE KIND OF PERSON I WOULD LIKE TO GET MARRIED TO. I DON'T EVEN KNOW HIM!

MAMA: KOUMBA! KOUMBA! KOUMBA! HOW MANY TIMES DID I CALL YOU?

KOUMBA: THREE TIMES.

MAMA: NOW LISTEN TO ME. AT YOUR AGE, IT IS DIFFICULT FOR YOU TO FIND SOMEONE WHO IS NOT MARRIED. ADAMU IS RICH AND IS NOT THE TYPE OF MAN THAT WILL BE AFTER YOUR MONEY. HE HAS HIS OWN MONEY.

WE JUST WANT YOU TO HAVE CHILDREN NOW BEFORE IT IS TOO LATE.

KOUMBA: (SPEAKING TO HERSELF) I DID NOT WANT TO GET MARRIED, BECAUSE I WAS AGAINST THE IDEA OF HAVING TO STAY AT HOME AND WAIT FOR A MAN, COOK FOR HIM, AND KNOW HE HAS MANY MISTRESSES AND NOT BE ABLE TO DO ANYTHING ABOUT IT.

SO, I REFUSED TO GET MARRIED. NOW THAT MY THIRTY-FIFTH BIRTHDAY IS APPROACHING, MY FAMILY WANTS TO FIND ME A MAN WHO IS NOT YET MARRIED, BUT BECAUSE OF MY AGE, IT IS ALMOST IMPOSSIBLE TO FIND A MAN WHO HAS NOT YET MARRIED, AND HE'S OLDER THAN THIRTY-FIVE.

NOW MY PARENTS FINALLY FOUND AND INTRO-DUCED ME TO A WELL-KNOWN BANKER, WHO HAS THREE OTHER WIVES AND FIFTEEN CHIL-DREN. OH! MY GOD!

I REFUSE TO GO BLINDLY INTO THIS RELATION-SHIP. THE IDEA OF BEING THE FOURTH WIFE SCARES ME SO MUCH BECAUSE OF THE DANGER THAT IT COMPRISES.

FINALLY, I REALLY DO NOT HAVE ANY CHOICE BUT TO MEET WITH THIS BANKER TOMORROW. THAT WILL REALLY MAKE MY PARENTS HAPPY. WHO KNOWS, I MIGHT BE ABLE TO HAVE AT LEAST ONE CHILD AFTER ALL.

THE NEXT DAY, KOUMBA GOES TO HER PARENTS' HOUSE AS PLANNED. SHE MEETS WITH ADAMU AND BOTH OF THEM RECEIVE KOUMBA'S PARENTS' BLESSINGS TO GET MARRIED.

KOUMBA IS ALSO IMPRESSED WITH ADAMU, WHO LOOKS DISTINGUISHED AND BRINGS HER A BIG GIFT ON THIS OCCASION. (A BRAND-NEW CAR.) ADAMU ALSO BRINGS A ROUND-TRIP WORLD TICKET ON THIS OCCASION AND PRESENTS IT TO KOUMBA, WHO IS MORE THAN FLATTERED.

ADAMU SHOWERS KOUMBA WITH GIFTS AND TRAVELS WITH HER TO ENGLAND, AMERICA, AND FRANCE ON FIVE DIFFERENT OCCASIONS IN JUST TWO MONTHS INTO THEIR RELATIONSHIP.

DURING THE SIXTH MONTH, KOUMBA GETS PREGNANT AND ADAMU DECIDES TO MARRY HER. THEY GET MARRIED TRADITIONALLY AND ACCORDING TO THE ISLAMIC RITES.

KOUMBA MOVES INTO ADAMU'S HOUSE. EIGHT MONTHS LATER, SHE GIVES BIRTH TO A BOUNCING BABY GIRL, ADIJA.

NOT ONLY DOES SHE NO LONGER GO ON EUROPEAN TOURS WITH HER HUSBAND, BUT NOW HER HUSBAND DOES NOT SLEEP IN HER BED

EVERY NIGHT. HE SLEEPS ALTERNATIVELY IN DIFFERENT BEDS EACH NIGHT.

EACH WIFE HAS HER OWN DAY THAT THE HUS-BAND WILL SLEEP WITH HER. KOUMBA'S DAY IS ON MONDAYS.

SINCE THERE ARE ONLY SEVEN DAYS IN A WEEK, EACH WIFE HAS A DAY FROM MONDAY TO THURSDAY THAT SHE HAS TO CHOOSE FROM.

FROM FRIDAY TO SUNDAY, ADAMU DOES NOT SLEEP IN THE HOUSE. HE GOES TO SLEEP OUT-SIDE WITH HIS MISTRESSES.

KOUMBA CANNOT UNDERSTAND THIS LIFE-STYLE, EVEN THOUGH SHE GREW UP SEEING IT IN HER OWN FAMILY; SHE REFUSES TO ACCEPT IT.

HER CO-WIVES FIGHT HER FOR EVERYTHING, AND ADAMU IS HER HUSBAND FOR JUST ONE DAY OF THE WEEK. "WHAT A LIFE," SHE KEEPS SAYING TO HERSELF ...

KOUMBA IS TIRED OF THIS LIFE AND WANTS OUT OF IT.

HER BOUTIQUE IS STILL IN SHAPE AND SHE STILL HAS HER CELEBRITY CLIENTELE.

SO, SHE MOVES OUT OF THE HOUSE OF HER HUSBAND AND GETS AN APARTMENT, WHERE SHE LIVES WITH HER DAUGHTER.

AT THE AGE OF THIRTY-NINE, AFTER A YEAR OF LIVING ALONE WITH HER DAUGHTER, THINGS BECOME DIFFICULT FOR HER. KOUMBA DECIDES TO LEAVE THE COUNTRY IN SEARCH OF A BETTER LIFE. SHE DECIDES TO GO TO AMERICA.

SHE TAKES HER DAUGHTER TO HER MOTHER'S, WHO UNDERSTANDS HER DAUGHTER'S MISERIES. IN ANY CASE, IT DOESN'T MATTER TO KOUMBA'S PARENTS ANYMORE. THEY WANTED HER TO HAVE A CHILD, AND SHE DID.

SO, KOUMBA SELLS EVERYTHING SHE HAS EVER LABORED FOR, GETS A TOURIST VISA, AND HEADS FOR WEST VIRGINIA, WHERE SHE HAD PREVIOUSLY CONTACTED A FRIEND, FATOU.

IT IS TRUE THAT SHE HAD VISITED AMERICA WITH ADAMU WHILE THEY WERE STILL DATING, BUT VISITING AMERICA THIS TIME AROUND SEEMS SO DIFFICULT THAT SHE IS SPEECHLESS.

WHEN KOUMBA GETS TO THE AIRPORT, SHE CALLS FATOU TO INFORM HER SHE IS IN AMERICA ... BUT SHE KEEPS GETTING FATOU'S ANSWERING MACHINE.

FATOU: HI, YOU MISSED ME. LEAVE ME A BRIEF MESSAGE AFTER THE TONE AND I'LL CALL YOU BACK.

KOUMBA: FATOU, HOW ARE YOU DOING? I ARRIVED AT THE AIRPORT TWO HOURS AGO, AND I AM STILL WAITING FOR YOU IN FRONT OF THE BRITISH AIRWAYS STAND. SEE YOU LATER.

(KOUMBA TRIES CALLING FATOU AGAIN.)

KOUMBA: HELLO, FATOU. I AM STILL IN FRONT OF THE BRITISH AIRWAYS STAND, AND I HAVE BEEN WAITING FOR YOU FOR FIVE HOURS NOW. PLEASE COME AND PICK ME UP. IT'S ME, YOUR FRIEND KOUMBA.

(KOUMBA TRIES CALLING FATOU AGAIN.)

KOUMBA: HELLO, FATOU. I AM STILL IN FRONT OF THE BRITISH AIRWAYS STAND, AND I HAVE BEEN WAITING FOR YOU FOR TEN HOURS NOW. PLEASE COME AND PICK ME UP. I AM EXHAUSTED, AND I AM HUNGRY. PLEASE COME FOR ME.

(KOUMBA TRIES CALLING FATOU AGAIN.)

KOUMBA: HELLO, FATOU. I HAVE BEEN WAIT-ING FOR YOU FOR ONE DAY NOW. PLEASE COME AND PICK ME UP. I AM EXHAUSTED, AND

I AM HUNGRY. PLEASE COME FOR ME. I HOPE YOU HAVE NOT TRAVELED. BUT YOU SAID I COULD STAY AT YOUR PLACE AND THAT YOU WERE GOING TO PICK ME UP. PLEASE COME FOR ME. I AM STILL AT THE AIRPORT. IT'S ME, KOUMBA.

(KOUMBA TRIES CALLING FATOU AGAIN.)

KOUMBA: HELLO, FATOU. THIS IS THE THIRD DAY I AM AT THE AIRPORT. I WILL GO AND CHECK INTO THE HOTEL AND CALL YOU FROM THERE. I DID NOT WANT TO DO THAT BECAUSE I DO NOT HAVE MUCH MONEY ON ME, BUT NOW I NEED TO GET SOME REST. I HAVE TRAVELED FOR EIGHTEEN HOURS, AND I HAVE NOT SLEPT.

I WILL CALL YOU WHEN I GET INTO THE HOTEL. IT'S ME, KOUMBA.

HOTEL RECEPTIONIST: HELLO. MAY I HELP YOU?

KOUMBA: YES, I WOULD LIKE A ROOM FOR THE NIGHT.

RECEPTIONIST: A SINGLE ROOM?

KOUMBA: YES. HOW MUCH IS IT FOR THE NIGHT?

RECEPTIONIST: $80.

KOUMBA: OKAY, I'LL TAKE IT.

RECEPTIONIST: HERE IS THE KEY. IT'S ROOM 105, ON THE FIRST FLOOR. HAVE A NICE STAY.

KOUMBA: THANK YOU.

KOUMBA GOES INTO THE ROOM AND SLEEPS ALL NIGHT BECAUSE SHE IS SO TIRED.

WHEN SHE WAKES UP THE NEXT DAY, SHE CALLS FATOU FROM HER HOTEL ROOM AND STILL CANNOT FIND HER, BUT SHE LEAVES HER THE ADDRESS OF THE HOTEL SHE IS IN.

(KOUMBA TRIES CALLING FATOU AGAIN.)

KOUMBA: FATOU, HERE I AM AGAIN TRYING DESPERATELY TO GET YOU. PLEASE CALL ME AT (772) 425-8856. THANK YOU AND BYE FOR NOW.

FATOU NEVER SHOWS UP TO GET HER.

AFTER THREE WEEKS IN THE HOTEL, KOUMBA RUNS OUT OF MONEY AND HAS TO LEAVE THE HOTEL TO AN UNKNOWN PLACE.

(KOUMBA TRIES CALLING FATOU AGAIN.)

KOUMBA: OH, MY GOD! WHAT AM I GOING TO DO NOW? I HAVE NO MORE MONEY AND MUST PAY AT THIS HOTEL DAILY. WELL, I GUESS I SHOULD LEAVE BEFORE I GET ARRESTED FOR NOT PAYING.

KOUMBA: HELLO, MISS. I WILL BE CHECKING OUT TODAY. HERE IS THE KEY TO THE ROOM.

RECEPTIONIST: OKAY. LET ME CHECK YOUR BALANCE. YOU ARE OKAY. YOU OWE NOTHING. THANK YOU FOR LODGING IN OUR HOTEL AND HAVE A NICE DAY.

KOUMBA: THANK YOU, AND SAME TO YOU. ("A NICE DAY WISH, THAT'S EXACTLY WHAT I NEED," SHE THINKS.)

KOUMBA TAKES HER BOX AND LEAVES THE HOTEL.

KOUMBA IS ON HER FEET ALL DAY. IT IS LATE AND SHE IS SLEEPY.

KOUMBA: WHERE AM I GOING TO SLEEP NOW? I HAVE NO MONEY TO GO TO THE HOTEL.

SHE FINDS A HIDDEN PLACE UNDER THE BRIDGE.

KOUMBA: I GUESS I COULD JUST SPEND THE NIGHT HERE.

SHE STRETCHES SOME OF HER CLOTHES ON THE FLOOR AND LIES ON THEM. SHE USES ONE OF HER BOO-BOOS THAT SHE BROUGHT FROM AFRICA TO COVER HERSELF. AROUND 1:00 AM, A POLICE VEHICLE PULLS OVER.

POLICEMAN: HELLO ... HEY! THAT'S NO PLACE FOR YOU TO SLEEP. GET UP AND LEAVE NOW!

KOUMBA: YES, SIR! I AM SORRY.

KOUMBA GETS UP, TAKES HER CLOTHES, AND KEEPS WALKING. SHE GETS DOWNTOWN AND MEETS SOME HOMELESS PEOPLE JUST LIKE HER. SHE HANGS WITH THEM FOR FIVE MONTHS.

UNFORTUNATELY FOR KOUMBA, THE COLD AIR OF WINTER HAS NOW STARTED BLOWING, AND SHE DOES NOT HAVE A WINTER COAT TO PROTECT HERSELF FROM THE COLD BREEZE OF WINTER. SHE DOESN'T KNOW WHERE TO GO AND CANNOT LOOK FOR A JOB BECAUSE SHE DOES NOT HAVE HER DOCUMENTS IN PLACE— NO WORKING PERMIT, NO SOCIAL SECURITY.

KOUMBA NOTICES THAT SOME OF THE HOME- LESS PEOPLE DISAPPEAR IN THE NIGHT AND SHOW UP AGAIN IN THE MORNING. SHE TRIES

*TO ASK THEM WHERE THEY GO AT NIGHT AND
NEVER REALLY GETS A CONCRETE RESPONSE.*

KOUMBA: HI, CHARLES AND RAY. HOW ARE
YOU BOTH DOING TODAY?

CHARLES: FINE, GIRL. HOW YOU DOING?

KOUMBA: ALL RIGHT, THANKS.

RAY: HOW ARE YOU DOING, KOUMBA?

KOUMBA: FINE, THANKS. SO, WHERE DO YOU
GUYS GO AT NIGHT?

RAY: SOMEWHERE ...

KOUMBA: WHERE?

CHARLES: WE GO HOME. WE BOTH LIVE IN
AN APARTMENT COMPLEX. WHAT ABOUT
YOU? WHERE DO YOU LIVE?

KOUMBA: I SLEEP HERE IN THE PARK.

CHARLES: OH! YOU DO? POOR GIRL!RAY: WELL,
YOU KNOW, YOU COULD GO INTO THE SHEL-
TER AND SLEEP THERE AT NIGHT.

KOUMBA: IS THAT RIGHT? WHERE IS THE
SHELTER?

CHARLES: COME, LET'S TAKE YOU THERE.

KOUMBA: YES, SURE, LET'S GO.

CHARLES: IT'S ABOUT TEN MINUTES FROM HERE.

KOUMBA: IT'S OKAY; I'VE GOT GOOD LEGS.

(THE THREE WALK TOGETHER FOR TEN MINUTES.)

RAY: DO YOU STAY ALL DAY AND ALL NIGHT ON THE STREET?

KOUMBA: YES, I DO. I REALLY DO NOT KNOW WHERE TO GO. I CAME FROM AFRICA SOME MONTHS AGO, AND MY FRIEND WAS TO PICK ME UP FROM THE AIRPORT—

RAY: WHAT HAPPENED? SHE THREW YOU OUT OF HER HOUSE?

KOUMBA: I WISH. SHE NEVER SHOWED UP AT THE AIRPORT. I KEPT CALLING HER HOUSE FOR THREE DAYS. I EVEN WENT AND LODGED AT THE HOTEL. THAT WAS WHERE I SPENT ALL THE MONEY I BROUGHT FROM AFRICA.

I RAN OUT OF CASH AND DECIDED TO LEAVE THE HOTEL BEFORE THEY THREW ME OUT. THAT'S HOW I ENDED UP ON THE STREET

AND HAVE SINCE BEEN LIVING UP AND DOWN THE STREET.

RAY: THAT'S SAD. SO YOU DO NOT KNOW WHERE TO SLEEP NOW?

CHARLES: THE SHELTER IS GOOD. BUT YOU WILL HAVE TO GET UP EARLY AND LEAVE. YOU ONLY GO BACK THERE TO SLEEP AT NIGHT.

KOUMBA: THAT'S OKAY. AT LEAST I AM GOING TO GET SOMEWHERE TO LAY DOWN MY HEAD AND SLEEP.

RAY: YES!

CHARLES: HOW DO YOU EAT?

KOUMBA: I DO NOT EAT ALL THE TIME. AT TIMES I BEG AND GET SOME MONEY FROM PEOPLE ON THE STREET ...

CHARLES: WAIT! YOU CAN GET FOOD FROM THE CATHOLIC CHARITY.

KOUMBA: OH YES?

CHARLES: YES! WE'LL TAKE YOU THERE AFTER.

RAY: HERE WE ARE. HERE IS THE SHELTER. JUST GET HERE AT 8:00 PM, AND YOU CAN SLEEP.

KOUMBA: THANK YOU. THE BUILDING IS NICE AND BIG.

CHARLES: AND IT'S WARM IN THERE.

KOUMBA: AND HOW DO YOU KNOW THAT? YOU USED TO LIVE HERE?

CHARLES: W-E-L-L- YE-ES AND NO!

RAY: WE BOTH LIVE HERE TOO.

KOUMBA: I THOUGHT YOU SAID YOU WERE ... WELL THAT'S JUST BY THE WAY

CHARLES: WE WERE JUST FOOLING AROUND. WE SLEEP HERE EVERY NIGHT.

KOUMBA: ANYWAY, THANK YOU FOR BRING-ING ME HERE.

RAY: NOW, LET'S GO TO THE FOOD PLACE.

KOUMBA: YES.

CHARLES: IT'S ONLY HALF A MILE FROM HERE.

KOUMBA: OKAY.

CHARLES: YOU CAN START RIGHT NOW. ARE YOU HUNGRY?

KOUMBA: YES, I AM.

RAY: WHAT TIME IS IT?

CHARLES: IT'S A QUARTER TO TWELVE.

RAY: THEY USUALLY SERVE LUNCH AT TWELVE.

KOUMBA: YES? SO WE WILL WAIT TILL TWELVE.

RAY: YES.

CHARLES: I THINK THEY ARE OPENING THE DOOR NOW.

KOUMBA: YES, LET'S GO!!! I'M STARVING.

ALL THREE WALK TOWARD THE DOOR. THEY GO INTO THE BUILDING AND SIT DOWN TO EAT.

RAY: LET'S GO GET SOME FOOD. YOU HAVE TO TAKE A TRAY AND GET WHAT THEY ARE SERV-ING FOR LUNCH TODAY.

KOUMBA: I SEE THAT.

CHARLES: WHAT ARE THEY SERVING? ... HMMM ... IT'S MASHED POTATOES AND ROAST BEEF. THAT LOOKS GOOD!

RAY: HMMM ... THEY HAVE CUPCAKES FOR DESSERT. JUST GRAB A TRAY, KOUMBA.

KOUMBA: THANKS.

THEY GET FOOD AND SIT DOWN TO EAT. WHEN THEY FINISH EATING, THEY ALL GO BACK TO THE PARK.

CHARLES: SO NOW YOU KNOW WHERE TO GO FOR LUNCH AND YOU KNOW WHERE TO GO TO SLEEP.

RAY: WE HAVE TO GO NOW.

KOUMBA: WHERE ARE YOU GOING?

CHARLES: AROUND ... LOOKING FOR BABES.

KOUMBA: OKAY, I UNDERSTAND. (LAUGHS)

RAY: BYE NOW.

CHARLES: BYE.

KOUMBA: BYE, GUYS.

KOUMBA WAITS IN THE PARK FOR THE REST OF THE DAY. AT 6:45 PM, SHE STARTS TO HEAD TOWARD THE SHELTER. SHE GETS TO THE SHELTER AND WAITS FOR THEM TO OPEN THE DOOR. THE DOOR IS OPENED AT 7:45 PM, AND SHE GOES IN AND INTRODUCES HERSELF TO THE ADMINISTRATOR. SHE IS ADMITTED IN THE SHELTER.

SHE GETS A BED TO SLEEP IN AFTER BEING ON THE STREET FOR SO LONG. THE ADMINISTRATOR EXPLAINS THE RULES AND REGULATIONS OF THE SHELTER TO HER. SHE MUST LEAVE THE SHELTER EARLY IN THE MORNING AND RETURN IN THE EVENING.

KOUMBA GOES TO HER BED AND FALLS ASLEEP IMMEDIATELY. IN THE MORNING, SHE GETS UP AS EARLY AS 6:00 AM AND GETS READY TO GO BACK ON THE STREET.

THE ADMINISTRATOR: HI, KOUMBA.

KOUMBA: HELLO.

THE ADMINISTRATOR: ARE YOU GOING ON THE STREET LIKE THAT? WITH NO COAT ON?

KOUMBA: I HAVE NO COAT. THAT'S WHY I WEAR AS MANY CLOTHES AS I CAN, TO KEEP ME WARM.

THE ADMINISTRATOR: WAIT, I THINK I HAVE A COAT AROUND HERE SOMEWHERE ... WHERE IS THAT COAT I SAW YESTERDAY ... THERE! HERE YOU ARE, KOUMBA. YOU CAN WEAR THIS.

KOUMBA: THANK YOU SO MUCH. (KOUMBA WEARS THE COAT AND LEAVES THE SHELTER.)

WHEN SHE LEAVES THE SHELTER, SHE ROAMS AROUND THE STREET, GOES TO THE CATHOLIC CHARITY FOOD BANK AT TWELVE, AND WAITS TILL THE EVENING TO GO BACK TO THE SHELTER TO SLEEP.

KOUMBA HAS LOST FIFTEEN POUNDS. SHE IS CONFUSED AND EVEN WANTS TO COMMIT SUICIDE.

BUT SHE TRUSTS GOD TO HELP HER OUT OF THIS SITUATION AND OFTEN SAYS TO HERSELF, "I AM GOING TO SURVIVE."

ONE DAY, TWO YEARS AFTER SHE'S COME TO AMERICA, STILL HOMELESS, STILL ROAMING THE STREETS, SHE GETS LUCKY.

SHE IS DOWNTOWN AND HAPPENS TO BE IN A PLACE WHERE A FILM PRODUCER, AARON, IS SHOOTING A FILM.

THE FILM PRODUCER DOES NOT HAVE ENOUGH FIGURANTS AND PASSERSBY.

THE PRODUCER: HELLO, MISS. DO YOU MIND REPLACING ONE OF OUR FIGURANTS WHO DIDN'T COME IN TIME?

IT WILL ONLY TAKE AN HOUR. ALL YOU HAVE TO DO IS DRINK A GLASS OF COKE AT THE BAR. YOU MUST NOT LOOK AT THE CAMERA. PRETEND YOU ARE NOT BEING PAID FOR THIS. CAN YOU DO IT?

KOUMBA: OH, YES, I CAN. YOU MEAN YOU WILL GIVE ME A HUNDRED DOLLARS FOR PARTICI-PATING?

THE PRODUCER: YES!

AT THE END OF THE SHOOT, THE PRODUCER IS IMPRESSED WITH HER PERFORMANCE.

THE PRODUCER: HELLO, MISS. THAT WAS GREAT! YOU DID EXACTLY WHAT I HAVE ASKED OF YOU. HOW WOULD YOU LIKE TO PARTICIPATE IN ANOTHER SHOOT I HAVE COMING UP IN A WEEK?

KOUMBA: THAT WILL BE GREAT! YES, I WOULD LIKE IT VERY MUCH.

THE PRODUCER: HERE IS MY CARD. CALL ME IN A WEEK SO THAT I CAN LET YOU KNOW WHEN EXACTLY YOU HAVE TO COME IN.

KOUMBA: OKAY, SIR.

KOUMBA IS SO HAPPY AND SAYS TO HERSELF: *"AMERICA IS REALLY THE LAND OF OPPORTUNITIES."*

KOUMBA IS SO HAPPY SHE GOT A HUNDRED DOLLARS JUST FOR SITTING IN A BAR, DRINKING A GLASS OF COKE. SHE RUNS TO THE STORE AND GETS HERSELF A NEW DRESS AND SOME UNDERWEAR.

BY THE TIME SHE HAS FINISHED SHOPPING, IT IS TIME FOR HER TO GO BACK TO THE SHELTER. SHE GOES BACK TO THE SHELTER AT NIGHT AND DOES NOT TELL ANYONE ABOUT WHAT HAD HAPPENED TO HER THAT DAY.

A WEEK LATER, SHE CALLS THE PRODUCER FOR HER APPOINTMENT, AND HE ASKS HER TO COME IN TO SEE HIM IN ANOTHER WEEK. THE APPOINTMENT IS ON A WEDNESDAY.

MEANWHILE, KOUMBA CONTINUES TO LEAD HER DAY-TO-DAY LIFE—FROM THE SHELTER TO THE FOOD BANK TO THE PARK.

A WEEK LATER, SHE GOES FOR HER APPOINT-MENT, TRYING TO LOOK HER BEST.

THE RECEPTIONIST: HI. MAY I HELP YOU?

KOUMBA: YES, I HAVE AN APPOINTMENT WITH MR. AARON.

RECEPTIONIST: LET ME NOTIFY HIM. WHAT'S YOUR NAME, PLEASE?

KOUMBA: MY NAME IS KOUMBA.

(THE RECEPTIONIST CALLS MR. AARON TO INFORM HIM THAT KOUMBA IS THERE TO SEE HIM.)

AARON: YES, LET HER IN.

THE RECEPTIONIST: OKAY, TAKE THE ELEVA-TOR TO THE THIRD FLOOR. HIS OFFICE IS #230.

KOUMBA: OKAY. THANK YOU.

KOUMBA KNOCKS ON THE DOOR AND GOES IN TO SEE MR. AARON.

AARON: HELLO, MISS. HOW ARE YOU DOING?

KOUMBA: FINE, THANK YOU.

AARON: PLEASE SIT DOWN.

KOUMBA: THANK YOU.

AARON CALLS HIS SECRETARY TO BRING IN A COPY OF KOUMBA'S CONTRACT.

AARON: SO HERE IT IS, MISS KOUMBA. LET ME BRIEF YOU ON THE PROJECT.

YOUR DUTY IS SIMPLE. YOU WILL HAVE TO APPEAR EVERY DAY FOR FOUR HOURS IN THE FILM THAT WILL LAST FOR FIVE MONTHS AND GET PAID $100,000.

WE WILL TRAVEL TO CALIFORNIA ON FIVE DIFFERENT OCCASIONS. YOU WILL BE GIVEN THE DATES AS THEY COME. DO YOU THINK YOU CAN HANDLE IT?

KOUMBA: YES!!! ABSOLUTELY! THANK YOU ... DID YOU JUST SAY $100,000? OR $1,000?

AARON: $100,000. THAT'S THE MINIMUM WE WILL PAY YOU FOR A FILM THAT LONG.

KOUMBA: THANK YOU SO MUCH AND GOD BLESS YOU.

AARON: YOU WILL HAVE TO SIGN A CONTRACT WITH US FIRST. HERE IS THE CONTRACT. YOU CAN TAKE SOME MINUTES TO READ IT.

KOUMBA: OKAY, SIR.

KOUMBA TAKES THE CONTRACT AND ONLY KEEPS READING THE AMOUNT $100,000 AND IGNORES THE OTHER PARTS OF THE CONTRACT.

KOUMBA: CAN I SIGN IT NOW, SIR?

AARON: HAVE YOU FINISHED READING IT?

KOUMBA: YES, SIR.

AARON: YOU CAN SIGN IT. YOU WILL START ON FRIDAY. THAT LEAVES YOU JUST TWO DAYS. MEET US IN THE PARK WHERE WE WERE THE FIRST TIME WE SAW YOU. BE THERE AT 7:30 AM. OKAY?

KOUMBA: OKAY, SIR.

KOUMBA CAN'T BELIEVE WHAT SHE HEARS. SHE BURSTS OUT CRYING. AARON DOESN'T UNDERSTAND WHY SHE IS CRYING AND ASKS HER WHY SHE IS CRYING. SHE NARRATES HER STORY FROM AFRICA TO AMERICA.

AARON FEELS SO SORRY FOR HER AND FEELS SO GOOD THAT HE IS ABLE TO HELP OUT SOMEONE WHO REALLY NEEDS HELP.

AARON: SO, WHERE ARE YOU GOING NOW?

KOUMBA: I LIVE IN THE SHELTER.

AARON: YOU DO? WOULD YOU LIKE TO GO OUT TO DINNER WITH ME?

KOUMBA: IT WOULD BE MY PLEASURE.

AARON GETS UP AND GOES TO HIS CAR WITH KOUMBA. HE TAKES HER TO A NICE RESTAURANT NEAR HIS OFFICE. AT DINNER, AARON DISCOVERS THAT KOUMBA HAS SO MUCH EXPERIENCE AND TALENT THAT COULD HIGHLY CONTRIBUTE TO HIS PRODUCTION.

AARON: SO, YOU WERE ONCE A RICH BUSINESSPERSON?

KOUMBA: YES! WELL, FOR AFRICAN STANDARDS. I KNEW EVERYBODY THAT WAS TO BE KNOWN IN AFRICA.

AARON: INTERESTING. DO YOU THINK YOU COULD WRITE A SCRIPT ON YOUR STORY?

KOUMBA: ABSOLUTELY. I LIVED IT. I CAN WRITE IT AS IF IT'S THE PRESENT.

AARON: OKAY, YOU GO AHEAD AND DO THAT. BUT YOU MIGHT HAVE TO WAIT TILL AFTER THE FILM IS OVER TO WRITE IT. YOU NEED TO CONCENTRATE WELL.

KOUMBA: NO PROBLEM. I WILL DO THAT.

AARON: SO, NOW, HOW DO YOU LIVE? DO YOU HAVE ANY FORM OF INCOME AT ALL?

KOUMBA: NO, I DO NOT.

AARON: OH! I FORGOT TO TELL YOU THIS. WE WILL GIVE YOU $25,000 BEFORE THE BEGINNING OF THE FILM, $25,000 TWO MONTHS LATER, $25,000 FOUR MONTHS LATER, AND $25,000, AT THE END OF THE FILM. IS THAT OKAY?

KOUMBA: OH! YES! IT'S MORE THAN OKAY. THANK YOU SO MUCH, SIR.

AARON: SO, YOU COME AND SEE ME TOMORROW IN MY OFFICE SO THAT I CAN GIVE YOU A CHECK.

KOUMBA: HOW DO I CASH THE CHECK?

AARON: YOU CAN TAKE IT TO ANY CHECK-CASHING PLACE, OR YOU CAN LEAVE IT IN YOUR ACCOUNT.

KOUMBA: DO I NEED TO PRESENT A FORM OF ID AT THE CHECK-CASHING PLACE?

AARON: YES, I BELIEVE SO.

KOUMBA: I DO NOT HAVE AN ID.

AARON: THEN YOU COULD LEAVE IT IN YOUR ACCOUNT.

THE WAITRESS: HELLO. ARE YOU READY TO ORDER DINNER?

AARON: WHAT GOOD MEAL HAVE YOU GOT FOR TONIGHT?

THE WAITRESS: WE HAVE LASAGNA.

AARON: HAVE YOU GOT FRENCH MEALS ON THE MENU TODAY?

THE WAITRESS: YES, LET ME GET YOU THE CARTE. HERE YOU ARE. WOULD YOU LIKE SOMETHING TO DRINK?

AARON: YES, THANK YOU. LET'S HAVE A BOTTLE OF SANCERRE ROSE. KOUMBA, DO YOU DRINK WINE?

KOUMBA: YES, I DO. SANCERRE ROSE IS A VERY GOOD CHOICE.

AARON: LET'S HAVE THAT.

THE WAITRESS: OKAY.

AARON: YOU KNOW ABOUT WINE TOO?

KOUMBA: YES, MY COUNTRY WAS COLO-
NIZED BY THE FRENCH, AND YOU KNOW THE
FRENCH ARE WELL KNOWN FOR THEIR GOOD
WINE. THAT'S PART OF THEIR CULTURE THEY
TRANSMITTED TO US.

AARON: YES, THAT'S TRUE. BENIN WAS COLO-
NIZED BY THE FRENCH.

KOUMBA: YES, WE WERE. THE FRENCH
CULTURE IS A VERY RICH ONE. I LOVE THE
FRENCH.

AARON: SO, THAT MEANS YOU SPEAK FRENCH
IN YOUR COUNTRY. THAT'S TRUE! SO, WHERE
DID YOU LEARN ENGLISH?

KOUMBA: I TOOK ENGLISH LESSONS IN HIGH
SCHOOL AND HAD ENOUGH CHANCES TO
PRACTICE IT BECAUSE I HAD SOME ENGLISH-
SPEAKING CLIENTS FOR MY FASHION DESIGN
STORE BACK IN AFRICA. I SPOKE ENGLISH
ALMOST EVERY DAY FOR MANY YEARS. NOW,
I SPEAK IT FLUENTLY.

AARON: YOU SOUND AS IF YOU WERE BORN
ENGLISH.

KOUMBA: THANK YOU.

AARON: NOW, LET'S GO BACK TO CASHING YOUR MONEY ... YOU KNOW YOU COULD LEAVE IT IN YOUR ACCOUNT?

KOUMBA: I KNOW, BUT I DO NOT HAVE AN ACCOUNT.

AARON: WELL! HMM! COME OVER TO THE OFFICE TOMORROW, AND WE'LL FIGURE SOMETHING OUT.

KOUMBA: WHAT TIME DO YOU WANT ME TO COME?

AARON: YOU COULD COME IN ANYTIME BETWEEN 2:00 PM AND 4:00 PM.

KOUMBA: I'LL BE THERE TOMORROW.

AARON: SO, TELL ME A BIT MORE ABOUT YOURSELF ...

KOUMBA: YOU WANT ME TO TELL YOU MY FULL HISTORY?

AARON: YES, YOU COULD. DOES IT BOTHER YOU?

KOUMBA: NO, IT DOES NOT BOTHER ME. I WAS JUST THINKING IT WOULD TAKE A WHOLE WEEK IF I HAVE TO TELL YOU MY FULL HISTORY.

AARON: THAT MUCH?

KOUMBA: YOU WILL BE SURPRISED!

AARON: LET'S HEAR IT.

KOUMBA: ARE YOU SURE?

AARON: YES, WE HAVE ALL NIGHT AT LEAST ... (LAUGHS)

KOUMBA: WELL, I HOPE I WON'T BORE YOU TO DEATH ...

AARON: YOU WON'T.

KOUMBA: OKAY, YOU ASKED FOR IT. IT ALL STARTED WHEN ...

(AT THE AGE OF FORTY YEARS, KOUMBA LEFT HER WEST AFRICAN COUNTRY IN SEARCH OF A BETTER LIFE IN AMERICA.

BEFORE SHE LEFT COTONOU, SHE WAS A TAILOR FOR FIVE YEARS. INITIALLY, SHE HAD IT ROUGH, AND OVER THE YEARS, SHE HAS HAD TIME TO BUILD UP HER CLIENTELE.

SHE SEWED BOO-BOOS (BEAUTIFUL AFRICAN WOMEN'S RELAX FITTING DRESSES) FOR THE WIVES OF THE PRESIDENT AND MINISTERS. LATER ON, SHE WAS KNOWN AS THE BEST COU-

TURIER IN THE WHOLE REPUBLIC OF BENIN, IN TOGO, IN NIGERIA, IN CAMEROON, IN GHANA ...

KOUMBA BECAME THE NUMBER ONE FASHION DESIGNER IN THE ENTIRE REGION OF WEST AFRICA.

AT THE AGE OF THIRTY-FOUR YEARS OLD, HER FAMILY FELT IT WAS TIME FOR HER TO GET MARRIED AND SETTLE DOWN WITH A MAN, INSTEAD OF CHANGING FROM ONE MAN TO ANOTHER.

SHE DID NOT WANT TO GET MARRIED BECAUSE SHE WAS AGAINST THE IDEA OF HAVING TO STAY AT HOME AND WAIT FOR A MAN, COOK FOR HIM, AND KNOW THAT HE HAS MANY MIS-TRESSES AND NOT BE ABLE TO DO ANYTHING ABOUT IT.

SO, SHE REFUSED TO GET MARRIED.

THE WAITRESS: EXCUSE ME. HERE IS YOUR DINNER. ENJOY YOUR MEAL.

AARON: THANK YOU.

KOUMBA: THANK YOU.

AARON: YOU ARE GOING TO LOVE THIS.

KOUMBA: I AM SURE. IT SMELLS GOOD TOO. HMM...

AARON: I ENJOY YOUR STORY; PLEASE CONTINUE.

SO, AS I WAS SAYING, A MONTH BEFORE HER THIRTY-FIFTH BIRTHDAY, HER FAMILY TRIED TO FIND HER A MAN WHO WAS NOT YET MARRIED, BUT BECAUSE OF HER AGE, IT WAS ALMOST IMPOSSIBLE TO FIND HER A MAN WHO WAS NOT MARRIED.

HER FAMILY FINALLY FOUND AND INTRODUCED HER TO A WELL-KNOWN BANKER, WHO HAD THREE OTHER WIVES AND FIFTEEN CHILDREN.

SHE REFUSED TO GO BLINDLY INTO THIS RELATIONSHIP. THE IDEA OF BEING THE FOURTH WIFE SCARED HER SO MUCH BECAUSE OF THE DANGER THAT IT IMPLIED.

FINALLY, SHE ACCEPTED, BECAUSE THE BANKER, ADAMU, SHOWERED HER WITH GIFTS AND TRAVELED WITH HER TO ENGLAND, AMERICA, AND FRANCE ON FIVE OCCASIONS IN JUST EIGHT MONTHS OF THEIR RELATIONSHIP.

DURING THE NINTH MONTH, KOUMBA GOT PREGNANT, AND ADAMU DECIDED TO MARRY HER. THEY GOT MARRIED TRADITIONALLY

AND ACCORDING TO THE ISLAMIC RITES, AND KOUMBA MOVED INTO ADAMU'S HOUSE.

EIGHT MONTHS LATER, SHE GAVE BIRTH TO A BOUNCING BABY GIRL, ADIJA.

NOT ONLY DID SHE NO LONGER GO ON EURO-PEAN TOURS WITH HER HUSBAND, BUT NOW, HER HUSBAND DID NOT SLEEP IN HER BED EVERY NIGHT. HE SLEPT ALTERNATIVELY IN DIF-FERENT BEDS EACH NIGHT.

EACH WIFE HAD HER OWN DAY THAT THE HUS-BAND WOULD SLEEP WITH HER. KOUMBA'S DAY WAS ON MONDAYS.

SINCE THERE WERE ONLY SEVEN DAYS IN A WEEK, EACH WIFE HAD A DAY FROM MONDAY TO THURSDAY. FROM FRIDAY TO SUNDAY, ADAMU DID NOT SLEEP IN THE HOUSE.

HE WENT TO SLEEP OUTSIDE WITH HIS MIS-TRESSES.

KOUMBA COULD NOT UNDERSTAND THIS LIFE-STYLE, EVEN THOUGH SHE GREW UP SEEING IT IN HER OWN FAMILY; SHE REFUSED TO ACCEPT IT.

HER CO-WIVES WOULD FIGHT HER FOR EVERY-THING. ADAMU WAS HER HUSBAND FOR JUST ONE DAY OF THE WEEK.

KOUMBA WAS TIRED OF THIS LIFE AND WANTED OUT OF IT.

HER BOUTIQUE WAS STILL IN SHAPE, AND SHE STILL HAD HER CELEBRITY CLIENTELE.

SO, SHE MOVED OUT OF THE HOUSE OF HER HUSBAND AND GOT AN APARTMENT, WHERE SHE LIVED WITH HER DAUGHTER.

AFTER A YEAR OF LIVING ALONE WITH HER DAUGHTER, THINGS BECAME DIFFICULT FOR HER AT THE AGE OF THIRTY-NINE. KOUMBA DECIDED TO LEAVE THE COUNTRY IN SEARCH OF A BETTER LIFE. SHE DECIDED TO GO TO AMERICA.

SHE GAVE HER DAUGHTER TO HER MOTHER. SHE SOLD EVERYTHING SHE HAD EVER LABORED FOR, TO GATHER MONEY TOGETHER FOR HER VISA AND TICKET FOR AMERICA.

SHE GOT A TOURIST VISA AND HEADED FOR WEST VIRGINIA, WHERE SHE HAD A FRIEND, FATOU.

SHE VISITED AMERICA WITH ADAMU WHILE THEY WERE STILL DATING, BUT VISITING AMER-ICA ALONE SEEMED SO DIFFICULT THAT SHE WAS SPEECHLESS.

WHEN KOUMBA GOT TO THE AIRPORT, SHE CALLED FATOU TO INFORM HER SHE WAS IN AMERICA ... BUT KEPT GETTING HER ANSWERING MACHINE.

FATOU: HI, YOU MISSED ME. LEAVE ME A BRIEF MESSAGE AFTER THE TONE, AND I'LL CALL YOU BACK ...

KOUMBA: FATOU, HOW ARE YOU DOING? I ARRIVED AT THE AIRPORT TWO HOURS AGO, AND I AM STILL WAITING FOR YOU IN FRONT OF THE BRITISH AIRWAYS STAND. SEE YOU LATER.

KOUMBA: HELLO, FATOU. I AM STILL IN FRONT OF THE BRITISH AIRWAYS STAND, AND I HAVE BEEN WAITING FOR YOU FOR FIVE HOURS NOW. PLEASE COME AND PICK ME UP. IT'S ME, YOUR FRIEND, KOUMBA.

KOUMBA: HELLO, FATOU. I AM STILL IN FRONT OF THE BRITISH AIRWAYS STAND, AND I HAVE BEEN WAITING FOR YOU FOR TEN HOURS NOW. PLEASE COME AND PICK ME UP. I AM EXHAUSTED, AND I AM HUNGRY. PLEASE COME FOR ME.

KOUMBA: HELLO, FATOU. I HAVE BEEN WAITING FOR YOU FOR ONE DAY NOW. PLEASE COME AND PICK ME UP. I AM EXHAUSTED, AND I AM HUNGRY. PLEASE COME FOR ME. I HOPE YOU HAVE NOT TRAVELED. BUT YOU SAID I COULD STAY AT YOUR PLACE AND THAT YOU WERE

GOING TO PICK ME UP. PLEASE COME FOR ME. I AM STILL AT THE AIRPORT. IT'S ME, KOUMBA.

KOUMBA: HELLO, FATOU. THIS IS THE THIRD DAY I AM AT THE AIRPORT. I WILL GO AND CHECK IN TO THE HOTEL AND CALL YOU FROM THERE. I DID NOT WANT TO DO THAT BECAUSE I DO NOT HAVE MUCH MONEY ON ME, BUT NOW, I NEED TO GET SOME REST. I HAVE TRAVELED FOR EIGHTEEN HOURS, AND I HAVE NOT SLEPT. I WILL CALL YOU WHEN I GET IN TO THE HOTEL. IT'S ME, KOUMBA.

HOTEL RECEPTIONIST: HELLO. MAY I HELP YOU?

KOUMBA: YES, I WOULD LIKE A ROOM FOR THE NIGHT.

RECEPTIONIST: A SINGLE ROOM?

KOUMBA: YES. HOW MUCH IS IT FOR THE NIGHT?

RECEPTIONIST: $80.

KOUMBA: OKAY, I'LL TAKE IT.

RECEPTIONIST: HERE IS THE KEY. IT'S ROOM 105, ON THE FIRST FLOOR. HAVE A NICE STAY.

KOUMBA: THANK YOU.

KOUMBA WENT INTO THE ROOM AND SLEPT ALL NIGHT BECAUSE SHE WAS SO TIRED.

WHEN SHE WOKE UP THE NEXT DAY, SHE CALLED FATOU FROM HER HOTEL ROOM AND STILL COULDN'T FIND HER, BUT LEFT HER THE ADDRESS OF THE HOTEL SHE WAS IN.

FATOU NEVER SHOWED UP TO GET HER.

AFTER THREE WEEKS IN THE HOTEL, KOUMBA RAN OUT OF MONEY AND HAD TO LEAVE THE HOTEL TO AN UNKNOWN PLACE.

SHE WAS HOMELESS FOR FIVE MONTHS, DIDN'T HAVE A WINTER COAT TO PROTECT HERSELF FROM THE COLD BREEZE OF WINTER, DIDN'T KNOW WHERE TO GO, AND COULDN'T LOOK FOR A JOB BECAUSE SHE DID NOT HAVE HER DOCUMENTS IN PLACE—NO WORKING PERMIT, NO SOCIAL SECURITY.

WHILE SHE WAS ON THE STREET, KOUMBA MET SOME HOMELESS GUYS WHO TOLD HER SHE COULD GO TO SLEEP IN A SHELTER.

SHE ALLOWED THEM TO TAKE HER THERE. IN THE SHELTER, SHE HAD TO LEAVE EARLY IN THE MORNING AND COME BACK AT NIGHT, JUST TO SLEEP.

WHEN SHE LEFT THE SHELTER, SHE ROAMED AROUND THE STREET AND BEGGED PEOPLE FOR MONEY. MOST OF THE TIME, NO ONE GAVE HER MONEY.

KOUMBA HAD LOST FIFTEEN POUNDS. SHE WAS CONFUSED AND EVEN WANTED TO COMMIT SUICIDE.

BUT SHE TRUSTED GOD TO HELP HER OUT OF THIS SITUATION AND OFTEN SAID TO HERSELF, "I AM GOING TO SURVIVE."

ONE DAY, TWO YEARS AFTER SHE'D COME TO AMERICA, STILL HOMELESS, STILL ROAMING THE STREETS, SHE MET LUCK.

SHE WAS DOWNTOWN AND HAPPENED TO BE IN A PLACE WHERE A FILM PRODUCER, AARON, WAS SHOOTING A FILM.

THE FILM PRODUCER DID NOT HAVE ENOUGH FIGURANTS AND PASSERSBY.

HE CALLED HER OVER AND ASKED HER IF SHE COULD PARTICIPATE IN THE PRODUCTION FOR AN HOUR, JUST SITTING AT THE BAR.

SHE ACCEPTED AND GOT A HUNDRED DOLLARS FOR HER PARTICIPATION.

AT THE END OF THE SHOOTING, THE PRODUCER WAS IMPRESSED WITH HER PERFORMANCE.

HE ASKED HER IF SHE WOULD LIKE TO WORK WITH HIM IN ANOTHER FILM THAT WAS COMING UP SOON.

SHE ACCEPTED. HE ARRANGED FOR HER TO MEET HIM IN HIS OFFICE TWO WEEKS LATER TO SIGN A CONTRACT.

SHE WAS SO HAPPY AND SAID TO HERSELF: "AMERICA IS REALLY THE LAND OF OPPORTU-NITIES."

SHE WENT BACK TO THE SHELTER AT NIGHT AND DID NOT TELL ANYONE ABOUT WHAT HAD HAPPENED TO HER THAT DAY.

TWO WEEKS LATER, SHE WENT FOR HER APPOINT-MENT, TRYING TO LOOK HER BEST. WHEN SHE GOT TO AARON'S OFFICE, HE GAVE HER A COPY OF THE CONTRACT TO SIGN. SHE WILL APPEAR IN A FILM THAT WILL BE SHOOTING FOR FIVE MONTHS AND GET PAID $100,000.

AND NOW, YOU ARE ASKING ME TO WRITE A SCRIPT? ON MY LIFE HISTORY?

AARON: YES, I WOULD LIKE YOU TO WRITE A SCRIPT ON YOUR FULL LIFE HISTORY. YOUR LIFE IS SO FULL OF EVENTS, AND I AM SURE IT

WILL BE A BIG STORY AND AT THE SAME TIME A LESSON OF HOPE FOR AMERICANS.

KOUMBA: YOU THINK SO?

AARON: YES, I KNOW SO.

KOUMBA: THIS IS JUST TOO GREAT. I THANK GOD FOR THIS OPPORTUNITY OF MEETING YOU.

AARON: YOU BELIEVE IN GOD TOO?

KOUMBA: YES, I DO BELIEVE IN GOD.

AARON: SO DO I. WHAT CHURCH DO YOU GO TO?

KOUMBA: I WAS ACTUALLY A MUSLIM. MY PARENTS ARE MUSLIMS. BUT I BELIEVE THAT THERE IS ONLY ONE GOD, AND I LOVE WOR-SHIPING GOD IN THE WAYS OF CHRISTIANS.

KOUMBA AND AARON FINISHED DINNER, AND AARON TOOK KOUMBA TO THE NEAR-EST MOTEL BECAUSE SHE TOLD HIM IT WAS TOO LATE TO GO INTO THE SHELTER. HE LEFT HER THERE AND GAVE HER $100 TO PAY FOR THE MOTEL.

KOUMBA: THANK YOU SO MUCH, SIR, FOR THE DINNER AND A PLEASANT EVENING. SEE YOU TOMORROW.

AARON: SEE YOU TOMORROW.

KOUMBA WENT INTO THE MOTEL AND GOT HERSELF A ROOM TO SLEEP IN FOR THE NIGHT. SHE GOT UP EARLY AND LEFT THE MOTEL SO THAT SHE WOULDN'T HAVE TO PAY FOR THE NEXT DAY. SHE WENT TO THE PARK TO PASS THE TIME. AT 2:30 PM SHE WENT TO SEE AARON.

THE RECEPTIONIST: MAY I HELP YOU?

KOUMBA: YES. I AM HERE TO SEE MR. AARON.

THE RECEPTIONIST: OKAY. WHO MAY I ANNOUNCE?

THE RECEPTIONIST: MISS KOUMBA WOULD LIKE TO SEE YOU, SIR.

AARON: LET HER IN.

THE RECEPTIONIST: GO ON ...

KOUMBA: I KNOW WHERE HIS OFFICE IS.

RECEPTIONIST: OKAY. YOU HAVE A NICE DAY, NOW.

KOUMBA: YOU TOO.

KOUMBA KNOCKS ON AARON'S DOOR.

AARON: COME IN.

KOUMBA OPENS THE DOOR.

AARON: HOW ARE YOU DOING?

KOUMBA: FINE, THANK YOU, AND YOU?

AARON: FINE, THANKS.

KOUMBA: I REALLY HAD A NICE TIME LAST NIGHT. THANK YOU SO MUCH FOR INVITING ME.

AARON: THANK YOU FOR BEING MY GUEST. NOW, WE ARE GOING TO GIVE YOU CASH.

KOUMBA: THANK YOU, SIR.

AARON: HERE IT IS. YOU MAY COUNT IT TO MAKE SURE IT'S EXACT.

KOUMBA: NO, IT'S OKAY. I BELIEVE IT'S EXACT.

KOUMBA PUTS THE WHOLE AMOUNT IN HER BAG.

AARON: YOU WOULD HAVE TO SIGN THAT YOU ACTUALLY GOT $25,000 FROM ME.

HERE IS THE DOCUMENT YOU WILL NEED TO SIGN. SIGN HERE. (HE SHOWS HER WHERE TO SIGN.) SO, WE'LL SEE YOU TOMORROW AT THE PARK.

KOUMBA: (OVERWHELMED) I WILL SEE YOU TOMORROW AT THE PARK. HAVE A NICE DAY, SIR.

AARON: YOU TOO, KOUMBA.

KOUMBA LEAVES. SHE IMMEDIATELY CHECKS HERSELF IN TO THE HOTEL. SHE LEFT ALL HER BELONGINGS AT THE SHELTER AND NEVER GOES BACK TO GET THEM.

SHE GOES DOWN TO THE HOTEL RESTAU-RANT TO TREAT HERSELF TO A NICE MEAL AND A GREAT BOTTLE OF WINE. AT THE END OF DINNER, SHE GOES UP TO HER ROOM AND SLEEPS. SHE DOESN'T WANT TO BE LATE FOR HER NEXT DAY JOB.

ON FRIDAY, SHE GETS UP AT 6:00 AM AND CALLS A CAB TO TAKE HER TO THE PARK.

SHE IS THIRTY MINUTES AHEAD OF TIME.

WHEN AARON GETS TO THE PARK, HE POSITIONS ALL FIGURANTS AND TELLS THEM TO CONVERSE WITH EACH OTHER FOR TWENTY MINUTES. THERE ARE SCENES WHERE THE FIGURANTS HAVE TO REACT TO THE EVENTS OF THE FILM.

AARON NOTICES THAT KOUMBA HAS SPECIAL ACTING SKILLS THAT NEED TO BE ENCOURAGED.

AT THE END OF THE SHOOT, AARON GOES TO KOUMBA.

AARON: YOU WERE GREAT!

KOUMBA: OH YES? THANK YOU, SIR.

AARON: HAVE YOU EVER ACTED BEFORE?

KOUMBA: NO, APART FROM WHEN YOU ASKED ME TO BE AN EXTRA IN THE FILM SHOOTING AT THE HARBOR TWO WEEKS AGO.

AARON: ARE YOU SERIOUS?

KOUMBA: ABSOLUTELY.

AARON: SO, WHERE ARE YOU GOING NOW?

KOUMBA: I WILL BE GOING TO THE HOTEL.

AARON: WOULD YOU WANT TO GO TO DINNER WITH ME AGAIN?

KOUMBA: I WILL BE DELIGHTED.

AARON: OKAY. HANG ON. LET ME ROUND UP WITH MY CREW MEMBERS.

KOUMBA: I'LL WAIT FOR YOU AT THE BAR.

AARON: OKAY, SEE YOU LATER.

KOUMBA WENT TO HAVE A DRINK AT THE BAR, AND AARON WENT ABOUT HIS BUSINESS WITH HIS CREW MEMBERS.

AARON: I AM READY; LET'S GO.

KOUMBA: OKAY.

AARON: WHAT DO YOU WANT TO HAVE FOR DINNER TODAY?

KOUMBA: I'LL LET YOU DECIDE.

AARON: WHAT ABOUT AN ITALIAN RESTAURANT FOR A CHANGE?

KOUMBA: THAT WILL BE GREAT.

AARON: COULD YOU WAIT FOR ME IN FRONT OF THE PARK? I'LL GO GET MY CAR.

KOUMBA: OKAY.

BOTH AARON AND KOUMBA WALK TOGETHER TO THE FRONT OF THE PARK, AND AARON GOES A SEPARATE WAY TO GET THE CAR; WHILE KOUMBA WAITS FOR HIM.

AARON: HI, MISS. HOP IN. (LAUGHS)

KOUMBA: HELLO!

KOUMBA GETS IN THE CAR, AND AARON DRIVES OFF.

AARON: KOUMBA, YOU WERE EXCELLENT!

KOUMBA: THANK YOU!

AARON: YOU MEAN YOU'VE NEVER ACTED BEFORE?

KOUMBA: NO, SERIOUSLY. THE FIRST TIME WAS WHEN YOU ASKED ME TO PARTICIPATE IN THE SHOOT.

AARON: THEN YOU HAVE AN ACTING GIFT ... (LAUGH)

KOUMBA: THANK YOOOU!

AARON: HERE WE ARE. YOU ARE GOING TO LOVE THIS RESTAURANT! THEY HAVE EXCELLENT MEALS ... AND GREAT WINE TOO!

KOUMBA: HMM! I COULD SMELL THE FOOD ALREADY.

AARON GETS OUT OF THE CAR AND LEAVES THE KEYS WITH THE PORTER. HE GOES AND OPENS THE DOOR FOR KOUMBA. THEY BOTH GO IN THE RESTAURANT AND ARE SEATED BY A WAITRESS.

AARON: IT IS WELL DECORATED IN HERE. I HAVE NOT COME TO THIS PARTICULAR RESTAURANT FOR FIVE YEARS. AND IT STILL LOOKS AS GOOD AS IT USED TO, EVEN BETTER. IT NOW HAS TWO STARS ...

KOUMBA: IT IS WELL DESERVED! THEY HAVE A PERFECT SILVER COLLECTION!

WAITRESS: HELLO. WOULD YOU LIKE TO HAVE A DRINK? (SHE BRINGS SOME SPICED OLIVES AND THE MEAL CARTE TO THE TABLE.)

AARON: OH! YES. CAN WE SEE THE WINE CARTE?

WAITRESS: YES, SURE. (SHE GOES AND GETS THE WINE CARTE.) HERE YOU ARE. I'LL LEAVE YOU A FEW MINUTES TO CHOOSE.

AARON: OKAY.

AARON: KOUMBA, YOU CHOOSE THE WINE. I KNOW YOU'LL MAKE AN EXCELLENT CHOICE.

KOUMBA: I'LL TRY.

AARON HANDS THE WINE CARTE TO KOUMBA, WHO TAKES HER TIME PERUSING THE WINES ON THE CARTE.

KOUMBA: WHAT ARE WE GOING TO EAT: MEAT OR FISH?

AARON: I'LL TAKE MEAT. THEY HAVE EXCELLENT BEEF.

KOUMBA: I'LL TRY THEIR MEAT TOO. SO LET'S TAKE A RED WINE.

AARON: OKAY! EXCELLENT CHOICE. WHICH WINE HAVE YOU CHOSEN?

KOUMBA: LET'S TAKE BOURGOGNE ROUGE.

AARON: OKAY, PERFECT WITH MEAT. EXCUSE ME, WE'VE CHOSEN A DRINK.

WAITRESS: OKAY. WHICH ONE?

AARON: BOURGOGNE ROUGE.

WAITRESS: OKAY.

AARON: THAT WAS AN EXCELLENT CHOICE.

KOUMBA: THANKS. I ALWAYS TRY TO MARRY THE MEAL WITH THE PERFECT WINE.

AARON: I CAN SEE THAT ... (LAUGHS! LAUGHS! LAUGHS!)

AARON: YOU KNOW WHAT, KOUMBA? YOUR LIFE HISTORY WOULD BE A PERFECT FILM, AND I AM SURE IT'S GOING TO BE A SUCCESS STORY ...

KOUMBA: YOU THINK SO?

WAITRESS: HERE IS YOUR WINE.

AARON: THANKS.

KOUMBA: THANKS.

AARON: OH YES! SO, TELL ME SOMETHING. YOUR DAUGHTER, ADIJA, IN AFRICA, WOULDN'T SHE MISS YOU? WHERE IS SHE LIVING NOW?

KOUMBA: SHE STAYS WITH MY PARENTS.

AARON: DO YOU SPEAK WITH THEM?

KOUMBA: I HAD IT ROUGH FOR SO LONG AND COULD NOT EVEN CALL THEM. BESIDES, THEY HAVE NO PHONE. I WILL HAVE TO EITHER WRITE THEM OR SEND A TELEGRAM. I WILL SEND THEM A TELEGRAM TOMORROW. THANK YOU SO MUCH, AARON, FOR TALKING ABOUT MY DAUGHTER. I MISS HER SO MUCH. I HAVE NOT BEEN THERE FOR HER WHEN SHE NEEDED ME AROUND. BUT YOU KNOW, I HAD NO CHOICE BUT TO TRY TO SURVIVE FOR ME AND HER ...

AARON: I KNOW ... DON'T EXPLAIN. I KNOW YOU ARE A LOVING MOTHER. BUT IN LIFE, THERE'S AN EXPRESSION: "YOU GOTTA DO WHAT YOU GOTTA DO!"

KOUMBA: I KNOW ... THAT'S WHY I DECIDED TO MOVE TO THE UNITED STATES ...

AARON: IT'S A GOOD CHOICE. I WOULDN'T HAVE MET YOU IF YOU DID NOT COME TO THE UNITED STATES.

KOUMBA: THAT'S TRUE ... I THANK GOD FOR MY LIFE ALL THE SAME. I HAVE LEARNT OVER THE PAST MONTHS THAT LIFE IS FILLED WITH GOOD AND BAD ... UPS AND DOWNS ...

THEY BOTH LOOK THROUGH THE MEAL CARTE.

AARON: YES! LET'S NOT BE SAD; LET'S ENJOY OUR EVENING.

KOUMBA: YES! I COULDN'T HAVE AGREED WITH YOU MORE ...

AARON: SO, LET'S ORDER FOR DINNER.

KOUMBA: BRILLIANT IDEA.

AARON: WAITRESS, EXCUSE ME, CAN WE ORDER FOR DINNER NOW?

WAITRESS: YES. WHAT WOULD YOU LIKE TO HAVE, MA'AM?

KOUMBA: I WOULD LIKE COURGETTE SALAD FOR A START, THEN SOME SPAGHETTI AND STEAK TARTAR.

WAITRESS: OKAY. WHAT ABOUT YOU, SIR?

AARON: I WOULD LIKE AVOCADO WITH SHRIMPS FOR A START, FOLLOWED BY STEAK AND LASAGNA.

WAITRESS: WOULD YOU LIKE SOME WATER?

AARON: YES! CAN WE HAVE SOME PERRIER WATER?

WAITRESS: ABSOLUTELY.

AARON: THANKS.

KOUMBA: I LOVE AVOCADO AND SHRIMPS; I COULD HAVE CHOSEN THAT.

AARON: DO YOU WANT HER TO CHANGE YOUR ENTREE?

KOUMBA: NO! I'LL TRY THAT SOME OTHER TIME.

AARON: YOU COULD TAKE SOME OUT OF MINE.

KOUMBA: YOU COULD ALSO HAVE SOME OF MY COURGETTE SALAD.

AARON: YOU'VE GOT YOURSELF A DEAL ...

KOUMBA: OKAY.

AARON: KOUMBA, ARE YOU STILL AFFECTED BY YOUR PAST RELATIONSHIP?

KOUMBA: I AM GETTING OUT OF IT BIT BY BIT.

AARON: YOU HAVE TO LET GO OF YOUR PAST AND MOVE ON.

KOUMBA: I KNOW. I AM TRYING HARD. BUT YOU KNOW IT'S NOT EASY TO LET GO OF THE PAST.

AARON: BUT IF I HANG OUT WITH YOU MORE OFTEN, IT MIGHT HELP ... (LAUGH)

KOUMBA SMILES.

KOUMBA: YOU MEAN YOU INTEND TO HANG OUT WITH ME MORE OFTEN?

AARON: IF YOU DON'T MIND MY COMPANY ... (LAUGH)

KOUMBA: NO, I REALLY DO NOT MIND YOUR COMPANY.

AARON: I GUESS THAT'S A YES!

KOUMBA: A DEFINITE YES ... (LAUGHS) ARE YOU NOT MARRIED?

AARON: I WAS, AND I GOT MY DIVORCE FOUR YEARS AGO.

KOUMBA: FOUR GOOD YEARS AND YOU'VE BEEN ALONE SINCE?

AARON: YES, I AM, JUST LIKE YOU. I I AM TRYING TO FORGET.

KOUMBA: YOU SEE, IT'S NOT VERY EASY TO LET GO OF THE PAST.

AARON: BUT WITH GOOD COMPANY IT COULD BE ...

KOUMBA: SO, YOU'VE NOT BEEN SEEING ANYONE SINCE YOU GOT YOUR DIVORCE?

AARON: I DID SEE SOMEONE FOR A YEAR, BUT SHE WAS SO MUCH LIKE MY EX-WIFE. I THOUGHT IT WAS BETTER FOR ME TO BE ALONE THAN GOING THROUGH THE SAME THING OVER AGAIN.

KOUMBA: I UNDERSTAND. IT'S VERY DIFFI-CULT TO WALK INTO ANOTHER RELATION-SHIP. ONE ALWAYS THINKS IT'S GOING TO BE THE SAME THING AGAIN.

AARON: NOT ALWAYS. BUT YOU USUALLY SEE IT IF IT'S GOING TO BE THE SAME THING OR NOT.

AFTER HAVING WORKED WITH KOUMBA ON SEVERAL OCCASIONS, AARON FALLS DEEPLY IN LOVE WITH HER, AND THEY BOTH DECIDE TO GET MARRIED.

THEY HAVE THE MOST BRILLIANT WEDDING, AND IT IS THE TALK OF THE TOWN FOR A WHOLE YEAR.

A YEAR AFTER KOUMBA GOT MARRIED, SHE HAS A SON (MARTIN) WITH AARON.

THEN KOUMBA DECIDES TO BRING HER DAUGHTER FROM AFRICA.

AARON AND KOUMBA MAKE THE BIGGEST FILMS AND MOVIES, AND HAVE AN ASSOCIA-TION THAT HELPS PEOPLE IN THE SHELTERS FIND THEIR WAY OUT OF THE SHELTER TO GET A BETTER LIFE, WITH A JOB.

AARON AND KOUMBA CHANGE THE NAME OF AARON'S PRODUCTION TO KOUMBARON PRODUCTION.

ONE DAY, KOUMBA GETS A VISIT. IT IS FATOU. SHE COMES INTO HER PRODUCTION STUDIO TO SEE HER. SHE TELLS HER SHE HAS BEEN WANTING TO SEE HER FOR A YEAR, BUT IT WAS IMPOSSIBLE, BECAUSE SHE KEPT GET-TING SENT BACK BY THE RECEPTIONIST.

KOUMBA IS SPEECHLESS. SHE TELLS FATOU THAT IT IS THANKS TO HER THAT SHE BECAME A SUCCESSFUL WIFE AND PRODUCER.

FATOU CAN'T UNDERSTAND HER. THEN KOUMBA NARRATES TO HER HOW SHE THOUGHT OF KILLING HERSELF WHEN FATOU HAD REFUSED TO COME AND GET HER AT

THE AIRPORT, HOW SHE RAN OUT OF MONEY, ETC. ...

FATOU THEN EXPLAINS TO KOUMBA THAT SHE WAS GOING THROUGH A HARD TIME.

HER HUSBAND HAD REFUSED TO ALLOW KOUMBA INTO THEIR HOME, WHICH WAS WHY SHE COULDN'T COME FOR HER AT THE AIRPORT.

KOUMBA FORGIVES HER AND INVITES HER AND HER HUSBAND TO THEIR HOME.

WHEN THE FATOU COUPLE COME TO VISIT KOUMBA, THEY HAVE AN INFERIORITY COM-PLEX THAT IS SO VISIBLE.

BUT KOUMBA NOTICES AND MAKES THEM FEEL AS COMFORTABLE AS POSSIBLE.

WHEN THEY FEEL MORE COMFORTABLE, THEY BOTH ASK KOUMBA TO HELP THEM OUT, BECAUSE THEY WERE THROWN OUT OF THEIR HOME BECAUSE THEY COULDN'T PAY THEIR RENT.

KOUMBA GIVES THEM $10,000 TO PAY FOR THEIRRENT AND ARREARS. OF COURSE, BEAUSE SHE GIVES THEM THAT AMOUNT OF MONEY, THEY KEEP COMING BACK FOR MORE MONEY. KOUMBA NOW THINKS THE

BEST THING SHE CAN DO FOR THEM IS TO PROVIDE AN EMPLOYMENT FOR THE COUPLE. OF COURSE, THISWILL BE A REGULAR CASH FLOW; IF THEY ARE SERIOUS ABOUT THEIR JOB...

SHE EMPLOYS THEM AT KOUMBARON PRODUCTION. THEY NOW BECOME A PART OF KOUMBARON PRODUCTION TEAM.

KOUMBA AND FATOU RECONCILIATE AND GET CLOSER THAN EVER. FATOU BECOMES THE ASSISTANT MANAGER IN THE HUMAN RESOURCES DEPARTMENT. HER HUSBAND IS THE DIRECTOR OF THE SECURITY SERVICES.

THINGS ARE JUST FINE BETWEEN THE TWO COUPLES, UNTIL FATOU DECIDES SHE WANTS AARON FOR HERSELF.

DESPITE ALL ATTEMPS FROM FATOU TO SEDUCE AARON, AARON JUST DOES NOT NOTICE. FATOU IS NOT GOING TO GIVE UP UNTIL SHE GETS HER BEST FRIEND'S HUSBAND FOR HERSELF.

AARON NOTICES ON TWO OCCASIONS THAT FATOU IS COMING ON TO HIM, BUT HE PRETENDS NOT TO NOTICE HER. AARON DOES NOT TELL KOUMBA ABOUT HER FRIEND'S REPUGNANT ACTION, BECAUSE HE DOES NOT

WANT TO CREATE CONFUSIONS BETWEEN THE TWO "CLOSEST FRIENDS".

ONE DAY, KOUMBA GOES ON A FILM TRIP FOR A WEEK. KOUMBA INFORMS HER BEST FRIEND.

KOUMBA :- BY THE WAY FATOU, I WILL BE GOING ON A FILM TRIP IN MEXICO. I WILL BE GONE FOR A WEEK. DO YOU WANT TO COME WITH ME?

FATOU :- NO, I WOULD HAVE LOVED TO GO WITH YOU, BUT I ALREADY HAVE SOMETHING PLANNED FOR THIS WEEK. I WILL GO WITH YOU THE NEXT TIME… HAVE FUN!!!

FOR FATOU, IT IS NOW OR NEVER TO GET AARON.

SOON AFTER KOUMBA LEAVES FOR HER TRIP, FATOU CALLS AARON TO "CHECK ON THE FAMILY, AND TO MAKE SURE THE KIDS ARE FINE".

AARON AND MARTIN ARE OUT IN THE PARK. BECAUSE SHE IS NOT ABLE TO SPEAK WITH AARON AND SHE DOES NOT WANT TO LEAVE HIM A MESSAGE, FATOU GOES TO THEIR HOME. SHE MEETS AARON IN FRONT OF THE HOUSE.

FATOU :- HELLO AARON, I HAVE BEEN CALL-
ING YOU ALL DAY TO CHECK ON YOU AND
MARTIN. I AM SO WORRIED THAT I DECIDED
TO DRIVE DOWN HERE MYSELF. SORRY TO
INTRUDE ON YOUR PRIVACY. I AM AFRAID
SOMETHING HAPPENED TO YOU AND THE
KID.

AARON :- THANK YOU FATOU. DO YOU CARE
TO COME IN FOR A DRINK?

FATOU AND AARON GO INSIDE THE HOUSE.

FATOU :- THE HOUSE LOOKS CLEAN, YOU AND
THE KID ARE DOING A GREAT JOB MAINTAIN-
ING THE HOUSE. KOUMBA IS GOING TO BE
HAPPY WHEN SHE COMES HOME. HER HOUSE
IS SPARKLING CLEAN.

(LAUGHS! LAUGHS! LAUGHS!)

AARON :- THANK YOU FATOU. WE ARE TRYING
OUR BEST.

(SILENCE! SILENCE! SILENCE!)

FATOU :- *(NOT SEEING THE KIDS)*, I AM HERE
TO CHECK PRINCIPALLY ON THE KIDS. I HAVE
NOT SEEN THEM IN A LONG TIME. *(SILENCE!
SILENCE! SILENCE!)* "WHERE IS THE KID"?

(FATOU WANTS TO BE SURE THAT THE KIDS ARE NOT IN THE HOUSE).

AARON :- HE IS PLAYING IN THE PARK. HE WOULD NOT WANT TO COME INSIDE NOW... HE IS PLAYING BASEBALL... HE LOVES B-A-S-E-B-A-L-L.

(SO, FATOU DECIDES THAT IT IS BETTER FOR HER TO ACT NOW. SHE LAYS ALL HER CARDS ON THE TABLE. SHE GETS UP FROM HER CHAIR, SHE RUNS AND SITS ON AARON'S LAP.

AARON :- FATOU, PLEASE S-T-O-O....

BEFORE AARON COULD COMPLETE HIS SENTENCE, WITH THE HOPE OF DESUADING FATOU FROM SITTING ON HIS LAP, FATOU GIVES AARON A FRENCH KISS. A REAL FRENCH KISS.

AARON LETS HIMSELF GO, CANNOT RESIST FATOU. FALLS INTO HER LONG SET TRAP, IN HIS MATRIMONIAL.   AARON LIFT FATOU UP AND TOOK HER INTO HIS MATRIMONIAL BED...

AFTER BOTH AARON AND FATOU REALIZED THEIR WISHES... FATOU SAYS TO AARON

FATOU :- I REALLY DO NOT WANT THIS TO HAPPEN, YOU ARE MY BEST FRINED'S HUSBAND. I CAN NOT BELIVE I JUST MADE YOU DO THIS... *(FATOU BREAKS DOWN IN TEARS).*

AARON :- I AM ASHAME OF MYSELF, BUT THAT'S LIFE.

FATOU :- I GUESS I SHOULD FEEL BETTER, BUT I REALLY DO NOT…

(AARON KEEPS QUIET AND STARES AT FATOU… FATOU RUNS INTO THE BATHROOM TO FRESHEN UP. WHEN SHE COMES OUT OF THE BATHROOM SHE WAS DRESSED. SHE SAYS TO AARON…)

FATOU :- AARON, I HAVE TO LEAVE…

(AARON KEEPS QUIET AND STARES AT FATOU… FATOU RUNS OUT OF THE HOUSE… FATOU HURRIES UP AND LEAVES THE HOUSE. ON GETTING TO HER HOME SHE CALLS AARON)

FATOU :- AARON, I AM SORRY THIS HAPPENED BETWEEN US, BUT I DO NOT REGRET ANY MOMENT SPENT WITH YOU.

AARON HANGS THE PHONE UP. THEN AARON THINKS OUT LOUD…

AARON :- I DO NOT REGRET ANY MOMENT WITH YOU EITHER.

(THE KIDS NOW WALK IN THE HOUSE)

MARTIN :- DADDY, WHO ARE YOU SPEAKING TO?

AARON :- TO MYSELF.

MARTIN:- DID SOMEONE JUST LEAVE HERE? SHE LOOKS LIKE FATOU...

AARON :- NO, IT IS NOT FATOU. IT IS A MAR-KETER WHO IS TRYING TO SELL SOME HOME EQUIPMENT.

(WHILE MARTIN AND DADDY ARE TALKING, SOMEONE PULLS UP AT THE DRIVE THROUGH. IT IS KOUMBA. THE KID HURRIES OUT OF THE HOUSE YELLING...)

KID :- MUMMY! MUMMY! *(MARTIN HUG HIS MOM.)*

KOUMBA :- I MISS YOU BABY. *(KOUMBA GIVES THE KID HIS GIFTS AND THEY HEAD TOWARDS THE DOOR. AARON IS LYING DOWN ON THE SOFA)*

KOUMBA :- HELLO HONEY! *(SHE GIVES AARON A KISS), BUT AS SOON AS KOUMBA WALKS IN, SHE NOTICES SOMETHING DIFFERENT IN AARON, BUT CAN NOT REALLY UNDERSTAND WHAT IT IS PRECISELY..*

AARON CAN NOT LOOK INTO KOUMBA'S FACE WHEN TALKING TO HER. KOUMBA THINKS MAYBE IT IS TIREDNESS, OR SHE IS JUST IMAG-INING THINGS).

KOUMBA :- AARON, I MISS YOU SO MUCH. HOW AREYOU? WHAT IS WRONG?.

AARON :- I MISS YOU TOO HONEY.

DESPITE AARON'S RESPONSE, KOUMBA STILL FEELS THAT SOMETHING IS STRANGE IN THE WAY AARON IS BEHAVING. KOUMBA SAYS TO HERSELF…

KOUMBA :- MAY BE I AM IMAGINING THINGS.

KOUMBA GOES UP TO THE BATHROOM TO TAKE A BATH. WHEN KOUMBA COMES BACK FROM TAKING A BATH AARON TELLS HER…

AARON :- I WANT TO GO OUT FOR A WALK.

KOUMBA :- ALRIGHT BABY. WHAT IS WRONG AARON? DID I DO ANYTHING WRONG?

THOUSANDS OF THOUGHTS GOES THROUGH KOUMBA'S MIND. "IS AARON ANGRY BECAUSE I WENT ON A TRIP"?, "IS HE ANGRY BECAUSE I DID NOT TELL HIM I WAS COMING HOME"?, "IS AARON ANGRY BECAUSE HE WAS LEFT ALONE WITH THE KIDS"?…, THOUSANDS OF THOUGHTS RUNS THROUGH KOUMBA'S MIND, BUT SHE DOES NOT WANT TO MAKE A BIG DEAL OF HER THOUGHTS. AARON COMES HOME TWENTY MINUTES LATTER AND IS STILL QUIET.

KOUMBA :- AARON BABY, WHAT IS THE MATTER?

AARON :- NOTHING BABY. I AM JUST TIRED... HOW WAS YOUR TRIP?

KOUMBA :- GREAT!!! EVERYTHING WENT AS PLANNED. WE JUST GOT THE $3BILLION CONTRACT FOR THE FILM MAKING...

AARON :- OH GREAT! WHAT ARE THE FILMING CONDITIONS REQUIRED AND WHEN WILL THE FILM SHOOTINHG START?

KOUMBA :- IN TWO WEEKS. WE HAVE TO RENT A CASTLE (RELAIS CHATEAU) IN THE SOUTH OF FRANCE. THEY CHOOSE FRANCE AND PARTICULARLY JEAN PIERRE CADET RELAIS CHATEAU.

AARON :- WOW! THAT IS BIG. JEAN PIERRE CADET. WHAT IS THE THEME OF THE MOVIE? DO YOU HAVE THE SCRIPT?

KOUMBA :- YES! WE NEED TO GO OVER THE SCRIPT TOGETHER. THEN WE CAN THINK ABOUT HOW THE METTEUR EN SCENE WILL EXECUTE IT.   I CONTACTED FRANCOIS RIGAUD IN PARIS TO START RECRUITING FOR CASTING...

AARON :- DID YOU SEND HIM A COPY OF THE SCRIPT?

KOUMBA :- YES. I ALSO REQUESTED FOR A QUOTE, BECAUSE I THINK IT IS BETTER THAT HE DIRECTS THE FILM, SINCE HE IS IN PARIS… WHAT DO YOU THINK?

AARON :- BRILLIANT. FRANCOIS IS THE BEST! YOU MADE THE RIGHT CHOICE…

KOUMBA :- HONEY, LET'S GO OVER THE SCRIPT AND THE FILMING CONDITIONS TOMORROW. I AM EXTREMELY TIRED. WHAT DO YOU WANT FOR DINNER?

AARON :- ANYTHING HONEY.

KOUMBA :- MARTIN WHAT DO YOU WANT FOR DINNER.

MARTIN :- I WANT SPAGHETTI.

KOUMBA :- DO YOU ALSO WANT SPAGHETTI AARON?

AARON :- YES THAT IS FINE THANKS.

SO KOUMBA GOES TO THE KITCHEN TO COOK DINNER. SHE ASKS THE KID TO COME AND HELP HER. WHEN DINNER IS READY, THE KID

SET THE TABLE AND KOUMBA CALLS EVERYONE TO DINE.

KOUMBA :- DINNER IS READY.

EVERYONE COMES TO THE TABLE TO DINE. AT DINNER, AARON STILL LOOKS STRANGE BUT KOUMBA IGNORES HIM. AARON AND THE KID TELLS KOUMBA WHAT HE DID WHILE KOUMBA WAS AWAY. AFTER DINNER, THE FAMILY SITS IN FRONT OF THE TELEVISION FOR A WHILE AND GO TO BED.

IN THE MORNING, AARON AND KOUMBA GO TO KOUMBARON PRODUCTION AND THE KIDS GO TO SCHOOL. AT WORK, KOUMBA, AARON AND THEIR PRODUCTION TEAM MEMBERS WORK AT HOW TO EXECUTE THE NEW MOVIE PRODUCT.

AFTER WORK, AARON TELLS KOUMBA THAT HE WANTS TO GO AND HAVE DINNER WITH SOME BUSINESS ASSOCIATES. HE TELLS KOUMBA THAT HE IS GOING OUT WITH TOM AND ANDRE. KOUMBA KNOWS THEM OF COURSE!!! AND SHE BELIEVES HIM.

KOUMBA :- WHAT TIME SHOULD WE EXPECT YOU BACK AT HOME?

AARON :- I REALLY DO NOT KNOW HONEY. YOU KNOW WHEN I SEE THOSE TWO CLOWNS WE PLAY BILLIARD FOREVER.

(THEY BOTH LAUGH :- LAUGHS! LAUGHS! LAUGHS!)

KOUMBA :- OH! I KNOW… WHAT A QUESTION. *(LAUGHS! LAUGHS! LAUGHS!)*

AARON :- YOU AND THE KIDS JUST GO TO SLEEP IF I DO NOT GET HOME EARLY ENOUGH.

(AARON KISSES KOUMBA AND LEAVES.)

KOUMBA :- SEE YOU LATTER OR TOMORROW MORNING HONEY.

AARON :- OKAY LOVE. I WILL CALL YOU.

AS SOON AS AARON LEAVES THE PRODUCTION COMPANY, HE CALLS FATOU.

AND TELLS HER TO MEET HIM AT HER HOUSE. FATOU HURRIES UP AND LEAVES FOR THE DAY.

AARON :- FATOU? GUESS WHAT?

FATOU :- WHAT?

AARON :- I AM ON MY WAY TO YOUR HOUSE, ARE YOU ON YOUR WAY HOME?

FATOU :- I WILL MEET YOU AT HOME.

AARON GETS TO THE FRONT OF FATOU'S HOUSE, AND WAITS IN HIS CAR TILL FATOU GETS HOME. AS SOON AS FATOU PULLS UP, AARON COMES OUT OF HIS CAR AND FOLLOWS HER TO HER APPARTMENT. BARELY HAD FATOU OPENED THE DOOR THAT AARON JUMPS ON HER.

SO, AARON AND FATOU KEEP SEEING EACH OTHER FOR EIGHT MONTHS BEFORE KOUMBA NOTICES THAT SOMETHING WIERED IS GOING ON BETWEEN FATOU AND HER HUSBAND. BUT THEN KOUMBA HAS DOUBTS ABOUT IT. THINK-ING OUTLOUD TO HERSELF...

KOUMBA :- HOW IN THE WORLD CAN I THINK THAT MY BEST FRIEND IS DATING MY HUS-BAND? THIS IS CRAZY! OUT OF MY THOUGHTS DEVIL!!!

IN THE MEANTIME, AARON AND FATOU KEEP SEEING EACH OTHER. THEY GET TOGETHER ON A REGULAR BASIS AT FATOU'S HOUSE. AFTER SEEING AARON FOR SO LONG, FATOU FINALLY DECIDES TO LEGALIZE THE SEPARATION BETWEEN HER HUSBAND AND HERSELF. SHE GETS A DIVORCE FROM HER HUSBAND.

ONE DAY KOUMBA AND FATOU DECIDE TO GO OUT FOR LUNCH. AT LUNCH, FATOU TELLS KOUMBA ABOUT WHAT SHE HAS DONE...

FATOU :- KOUMBA, I HAVE DECIDED TO GET A DIVORCE FROM MY HUSBAND. WHAT GOOD DOES STAYING MARRIED TO HIM DO ME?

KOUMBA :- WHY DID YOU GET A DIVORCE? I THOUGHT BOTH OF YOU WERE TRYING TO WORK THINGS OUT...

FATOU :- I WAS TRYING TO WORK THINGS OUT WITH HIM, BUT I GOT FRUSTRATED...

KOUMBA :- WHY?

FATOU :- HE WAS MESSING AROUND WITH MY NEIGHBOR. THE EMBARRASSMENT WAS TOO MUCH. THAT WAS WHY WE SEPARATED IN THE FIRST PLACE.

KOUMBA :- I AM REALLY SORRY TO HEAR ABOUT THIS. SO, ARE YOU SEEING ANYONE NOW?

FATOU :- NOT REALLY...

KOUMBA :- NOT REALLY? *(LAUGHS! LAUGHS! LAUGHS!)* WHO IS THE LUCKY GUY?

FATOU :- I WILL LET YOU KNOW WHEN THE TIME COME.

KOUMBA :- LET ME KNOW. *(LITTLE DOES KOUMBA KNOW THAT FATOU IS ACTUALLY MESSING AROUND WITH HER OWN HUSBAND).*

AARON TELLS HIS WIFE THAT KOUMBARON PRODUCTION NEEDS TO EXPAND. THEY BOTH AGREE THAT KOUMBARON PRODUCTION NEEDS TO EXPAND. FOR THAT, AARON TRAVELS TO MEET OTHER PRODUCTION COMPANIES TO CONTRACT NEW BUSINESS IDEAS.

SO AARON GOES ON BUSINESS TRIPS, MORE OFTEN THAN BEFORE. GUESS WHAT? THE BUSINESS TRIPS ARE AT FATOU'S HOME.

KOUMBA TRUSTS HER HUSBAND AND REFUSES TO BELIEVE THAT HER HUSBAND IS CHEATING ON HER. ALL OF A SUDDEN, KOUMBA NOTICES THAT FATOU IS PREGNANT. KOUMBA FEELS THAT FATOU WENT BACK TO HER HUSBAND. SHE ASKED FATOU...

KOUMBA :- LOOK WHO IS PREGNANT...

FATOU :- YES INDEED!

KOUMBA :- ARE YOU SURE OF WHAT SHE WANT.

FATOU :- ABSOLUTELY.

KOUMBA :- SO, WHO IS THE LUCKY GUY?

FATOU :- IT'S A SECRET.

KOUMBA :- YOU ARE NOT EVEN GOING TO TELL YOUR BEST FRIEND?

FATOU :- NOT YET. I WILL TELL YOU WHEN THE TIME IS RIGHT.

KOUMBA :- I HOPE AARON AND I WILL HAVE THE OPPORTUNITY TO MEET THE LUCKY GUY AT DINNER AT OUR HOME NEXT WEEKEND.

FATOU :- THAT WILL BE GREAT.

KOUMBA :- I WILL LET MY HUSBAND KNOW THAT YOU AND YOUR FIANCE ARE COMING FOR DINER ON SATURDAY.

THROUGH OUT THE WEEK, FATOU TRIED HER BEST TO AVOID TALKING TO KOUMBA ABOUT THE DINNER. KOUMBA CALLS FATOU AND ASKS HER IF THE DINNER STILL HOLDS. FATOU SAYS YES. ON SATURDAY, KOUMBA MADE DINNER, BUT FATOU AND HER FIANCE NEVER SHOWS UP FOR DINNER. KOUMBA CALLS FATOU, AND FATOU TELLS HER THAT SHE IS NOT FEELING WELL, AND THAT SHE IS SORRY. KOUMBA SAYS SHE UNDERSTANDS.

KOUMBA :- AARON, THIS IS STRANGE. FATOU SHOULD HAVE CALLED ME TO PREVENT ME FROM COOKING DINNER.

AARON :- MAY BE SHE IS NOT FEELING WELL.

KOUMBA :- THAT IS WHAT SHE SAYS.

BUT BEFORE KOUMBA CAN REALIZE THAT FATOU IS HAVING A BABY BY HER HUSBAND, IT IS TOO LATE.

AARON GOES ON ANOTHER BUSINESS TRIP AS USUAL, FOR A WEEK.

ONE DAY, WHILE AARON IS GONE ON HIS BUSI-NESS TRIP, KOUMBA IS BORED AND DECIDES TO PAY FATOU A SURPRISED VISIT. KOUMBA WANTS TO GO TO THE RESTAURANT AND NEEDS COM-PANY.

SHE DECIDES TO CALL FATOU. FATOU DOESN'T ANSWER HER PHONE FOR TWO DAYS. KOUMBA STARTS GETTING WORRIED AND DECIDES TO DRIVE DOWN TO FATOU'S APARTMENT. KOUMBA TAKES HER CAR AND DRIVE TO FATOU'S HOUSE. ON GETTING TO THE FRONT OF FATOU'S COM-PLEX, IN FRONT OF FATOU'S APARTMENT COM-PLEX, KOUMBA NOTICES THAT AARON'S CAR IS PARKED IN FRONT OF FATOU'S BUILDING. SHE SAYS TO HERSELF…

KOUMBA :- NO, IT'S NOT AARON'S CAR. IT LOOKS LIKE IT, BUT I AM SURE IT'S NOT HIS CAR. AARON IS SUPPOSED TO BE OUT OF STATE…

KOUMBA MOVES CLOSER TO AARON'S CAR AND REALIZES THAT THE SIMILARITY IS IMPOSSIBLE. WHEN KOUMBA GETS CLOSER TO AARON'S CAR, SHE SEES THE TAG AND SAYS, "MAYBE AARON CAME BACK EARLY AND STOPPED BY AT FATOU'S HOUSE TO GIVE HER THE SCRIPT OF A NEW RECRUIT."

KOUMBA GOES IN FRONT OF FATOU'S APART-MENT COMPLEX. WHEN SHE WANTS TO PRESS FATOU'S DOORBELL, SHE SEES SOMEONE COMING OUT AND DECIDES TO JUST GO IN AND SURPRISE FATOU.

WHEN KOUMBA REACHES FATOU'S FLOOR, SHE HEARS AARON LAUGHING BUT DOES NOT FEEL SOMETHING IS WRONG.

KOUMBA RINGS THE DOORBELL AND HEARS AARON SAY, "IT'S THE PIZZA."   AARON COMES TO ANSWER THE DOOR IN HIS BATHROBE.

KOUMBA CAN'T BELIEVE HER EYES WHEN SHE SEES FATOU HALF-NUDE COME OUT OF THE BEDROOM.

KOUMBA TELLS AARON AND FATOU THAT SHE NEEDS AN EXPLANATION FOR THIS BETRAYAL.

FATOU :- WE DO NOT OWE YOU AN EXPLANA-TION. WE ARE ADULTS, AND WE DO WHAT WE WANT."

KOUMBA IGNORES FATOU AND SPEAKS DIRECTLY WITH AARON…

KOUMBA : - AARON? WHAT IN THE WORLD ARE YOU DOING HERE?

AARON IS SPEECHLESS…

KOUMBA :- FATOU, I WOULD NEVER HAVE THOUGHT IN A MILLION YEARS THAT YOU COULD BETRAY ME. IS THE CHILD YOU ARE CARRYING AARON'S?"

FATOU :- YES! AND GUESS WHAT, WE ARE GOING TO GET MARRIED.

AARON IS STILL SPEECHLESS…

KOUMBA :- I CANNOT BELIEVE THIS.

KOUMBA LEAVES FATOU'S APPARTMENT, GOES BACK HOME AND CONTACTS HER LAWYER IMME-DIATELY TO FILE FOR A DIVORCE. WHILE SHE WAS ON THE PHONE TALKING TO HER LAWYER, AARON RUNS IN THE HOUSE AND BEGS KOUMBA TO PLEASE FORGIVE HIM.

AARON : PLEASE FORGIVE ME KOUMBA. IT IS A MISTAKE.

KOUMBA :- IS FATOU'S PREGNANCY ALSO A MISTAKE?

AARON :- PLEASE KOUMBA. I HAVE NO EXCUSE, BUT THIS IS AN HONEST MISTAKE.

KOUMBA :- AARON, FROM NOW ONWARDS, WE DO NOT HAVE ANYTHING ELSE TO SAY TO EACH OTHER. I WILL PLEASE ASK YOU TO LEAVE THIS HOUSE AND WITH IMMEDIATE EFFECT.

AARON :- PLEASE FORGIVE ME KOUMBA. *(KOUMBA NO LONGER RESPONDS AND AARON LEAVES THE HOUSE IN TEARS.)*

KOUMBA CALLS HER LAWYER BACK TO LEAVE HIM A MESSAGE AS SOON AS AARON LEAVES THE HOUSE. IN THE MORNING, HER LAWYER MEETS WITH HER, COMPLETE ALL PAPERWORK AND KOUMBA GETS HER DIVORCE FROM AAROM. KOUMBA GETS CUSTODY OF THEIR CHILD, KOUMBA GETS TO KEEP THE HOUSE, THE COMPANY KOUMBARON.

KOUMBA IS NOW THE SOLE OWNER OF KOUMBARON PRODUCTION.

AARON REFUSES TO SHOW THAT HE IS DISTURBED BY THE PRESENT SITUATION, IN WHICH HE PUTS HIMSELF. HE IS FINE WITH LIVING WITH FATOU AND THEIR NEW BABY GIRL. FATOU RESIGNS AT KOUMBARON PRODUCTION AND GETS A LESS PAYING JOB AT ANOTHER PRODUCTION COMPANY. AARON IS UNABLE TO FIND

A JOB, BECAUSE HE IS UNWILLING TO WORK UNDER ANYONE AUTHORITY.

AARON :- I AM JUST UPSET WITH MYSELF FOR LETTING GO OF EVERYTHING I HAD WITH MY EX-WIFE.

FATOU :- SEE! I TOLD YOU THAT YOU DID NOT HAVE TO TELL THE JUDGE THAT YOU ARE NOT INTERESTED IN HAVING ANYTHING. IT IS DIFFICULT FOR ME TO WORK HARD FOR YOU AND THE BABY ALL BY MYSELF.

AARON :- OKAY! UNDERSTOOD. IF YOU WANT ME TO LEAVE I WILL.

FATOU :- NO AARON, I AM JUST TRYING TO EXPLAIN TO YOU THAT IF YOU HAVE AT LEAST A QUARTER OF WHAT YOU HAD, I WOULD NOT HAVE TO WORK THIS HARD TO PAY OUR BILLS.

AARON GETS UP AND LEAVES THE APPART-MENT. AARON IS GONE ALL NIGHT. FATOU TRIES TO REACH HIM ON HIS CELLULAR, BUT AARON REFUSES TO SPEAK WITH HER.IN THE MORN-ING, AARON COMES BACK HOME. HE SLEEPS ALL DAY UNTIL FATOU GETS BACK IN THE HOUSE. AS SOON AS FATOU SEES AARON, SHE TELLS HIM HOW SORRY SHE IS TO HAVE UPSET HIM...

FATOU :- AARON, I AM SORRY AND DID NOT MEAN TO UPSET YOU YESTERDAY. I LOVE YOU AND I JUST WANT US TO HAVE A PLEASING FAMILY LIFE FOR ME AND OUR KID.

AARON IS NOT RESPONDING. FATOU LEAVES THE ROOM. GOES INTO THE KITCHEN TO COOK DINNER. SUDDENLY, FATOU SEES THAT AARON IS GETTING DRESSED TO GO OUT AGAIN...

FATOU :- AARON, WHERE ARE YOU GOING AT THIS TIME OF THE NIGHT?

AARON DOES NOT RESPOND. HE KEEPS GETTING DRESSED AND IS HEADING TOWARDS THE DOOR TO LEAVE THE APPARTMENT, THEN,...FATOU RUNS TO PREVENT AARON FROM OPENING THE DOOR AND LEAVING THE HOME. AS FATOU APPROACHES AARON, AARON PUSHED HER TO THE FLOOR AND HE LEAVES WITHOUT SAYING A WORD. THE NEXT MORNING, AARON COMES BACK HOME. THIS TIME FATOU IS HOME...

FATOU :- HELLO AARON... I AM HOME BECAUSE WHEN YOU PUSHED ME TO THE FLOOR LAST NIGTH, I FELL ON THE TABLE AND THE GLASS CUP ON THE TABLE FELL, BROKE AND HURT MY LEG. I WENT TO THE HOSPITAL AND GOT STICHES.

AARON :- FATOU, I AM SORRY. I AM JUST FRUS-TRATED WITH MY PRESENT SITUATION. I

WAS FINE WITH MY EX-WIFE AND MY FAMILY
UNTIL YOU CAME ALONG…

*AARON DID NOT GET A CHANCE TO FINISH THE
SENTENCE WHEN FATOU SAID…*

FATOU :- AARON? I CAN NOT BELIEVE YOU
JUST SAID THAT. DO YOU REMEMBER THAT
YOU CAME ON TO ME??? YOU KNEW I WAS YOU
WIFE'S BEST FRIEND, BUT YOU STILL CAME ON
TO ME. THEN YOU SAID YOU DID NOT REGRET
ANYTHING THAT HAPPENED BETWEEN US…
THEN AFTER THAT YOU MOVED INTO MY
APPARTMENT, I DID NOT ASK YOU TO MOVE
IN WITH ME…

AARON DOES NOT SAY A WORD…

FATOU :- THEN NOW, YOU ARE BLAMING
ME FOR EVERYTHING? I CAN NOT BELIEVE
YOU…

AARON DOES NOT SAY A WORD…

AARON :- I CAN NOT BELIEVE THAT YOU ARE
STANDING BEFORE ME AND SAYING ALL THAT.
NOW TELL ME, HOW LONG HAVE YOU BEEN
SEEING STEVE?

FATOU :- STEVE? WHO IS SEEING STEVE?
WHICH STEVE?

AARON :- PLEASE DO NOT PLAY AND PRETEND TO BE STUPID. I SPOKE WITH STEVE. BOTH OF YOU HAVE BEEN CHEATING ON ME FOR THE PAST FIVE MONTH. I HEARD ABOUT IT AND I FOLLOWED BOTH OF YOU ON ONE OF YOUR HOTEL GETAWAYS. AND YOU HAVE THE GUTTS TO STAND HERE BEFORE ME AND TELL ME THAT I AM...

FATOU :- I DID NOT WANT TO DO IT AARON. STEVE MADE ME DO IT.

AARON :- JUST AS I MADE YOU DO IT, BUT YOU HAD IT PLANNED. ALL YOU NEEDED ME FOR WAS TO EXECUTE YOUR WISH AS PLANNED. NOW I DO NOT HAVE A LIFE AND YOU ARE TRYING YOUR BEST TO FRUSTRATE AND DUMP ME...

FATOU :- HOW COULD YOU SAY THAT AARON?

AARON :- HOW COULD I SAY WHAT? THAT YOU HAD EVERYTHING PLANNED AND YOU JUST NEEDED STEVE TO HELP YOU EXECUTE YOUR WISH JUST AS YOU DID WITH ME?

FATOU :- AARON, I REALLY DO NOT UNDER-STAND YOU. PLEASE SIT DOWN AND LET'S TALK THIS OVER *(FATOU TRIES TO TOUCH AARON)*...

AARON :- DO NOT EVEN TRY TO TOUCH ME YOU... B... *(AARON LEAVES THE HOUSE WITH-OUT ANYTHING ON HIM FATOU DOES NOT EVEN TRY TO STOP HIM.)*

AARON DOES NOT KNOW WHERE TO GO, HE SLEEPS ON THE STREET FOR THE NIGHT. THE NEXT MORNING, AARON CALLS KOUMBA AT KOUMBARON PRODUCTION COMPANY.

AARON :- HELLO KOUMBA IT'S AARON.

KOUMBA :- AARON? WHAT DO YOU WANT?

AARON :- I NEED YOUR HELP

KOUMBA :- WHAT HELP? PLEASE DO NOT CALL ME AGAIN.

AARON :- I WILL TALK TO YOU LATTER. I AM SORRY FOR BETRAYING YOU. PLEASE FORGIVE ME.

KOUMBA :- OKAY

AARON :- PLEASE FORGIVE ME. I WANT TO COME BACK HOME.

KOUMBA :- COME BACK WHERE? WHICH HOME?

AARON :- I AM SORRY I EVEN ASKED YOU TO LET ME COME HOME. PLEASE TAKE CARE OF THE KID.

KOUMBA HANGS THE PHONE UP. AARON NOW HANGS UP. AARON NOW DECIDES TO GO OUT OF STATE. HE GETS INTO HIS CAR AND DRIVES FOR HOURS. HE SEES A BAR ALONG THE ROAD SIDE. HE COMES OUT OF HIS CAR, WALKS INTO THE BAR AND DRINKS FOR HOUR S. AARON GETS DRUNK, LEAVE THE BAR, AND DRIVES FOR FIVE MINUTES, THEN HE RUNS OFF THE ROAD INTO A DITCH. AARON IS RESCUED AND IS HOSPITALIZED FOR EIGHT MONTHS. FROM THE ACCIDENT, AARON BECOMES PARALIZED. HE IS SENT TO THE NURSING FOR REHABILITATION.

KOUMBA SPEAKS ABOUT THE PHONE CALL THAT SHE RECEIVE FROM AARON WITH HER NEW BOY FRIEND CHARLES.

KOUMBA :- WHAT IS GOING ON WITH AARON.

CHARLES :- WHAT DO YOU MEAN?

KOUMBA :- HE CALLED ME EIGHT MONTHS AGO, HE WAS ASKING ME TO HELP ME. HE ALSO SAID THAT HE WANTED TO COME HOME. I SAID NO WAY! SINCE THEN I HAVE NOT HEARD ABOUT HIM.

CHARLES :- I AM SURE THAT HE IS FINE WHER-
EVER HE IS.

KOUMBA :- I HOPE SO.

*KOUMBA THINKS TO HERSELF THAT IT IS
BETTER THAT SHE HIRES A PRIVATE DETECTIVE
TO LOOK FOR AARON. SHE HIRES A DETECTIVE
WHO INFORMS HER OF WHAT HAS HAPPENED
TO AARON. KOUMBA GOES TO THE NURSING
HOME WHERE AARON HAS BEEN STAYING. SHE
BRINGS HIM BACK HOME WITH HER. CHARLES
DOES NOT LIKE THE IDEA THAT AARON IS
LIVING IN THE HOUSE WITH THEM, BUT HE IS
UNABLE TO DO ANYTHING ABOUT IT.*

CHARLES AND AARON BECOME THE GREAT-
EST ENEMIES ON EARTH. CHARLES IS AFRAID
THEY MIGHT GET BACK TOGETHER, AND
AARON CANNOT STAND CHARLES BECAUSE
HE IS CONVINCED HE ONLY LOVES KOUMBA
BECAUSE OF THE WEALTH AARON HAD ACCU-
MULATED WITH KOUMBA BEFORE THEY BOTH
BROKE UP.

AARON TELLS KOUMBA TO WATCH OUT FOR
CHARLES' INTENTIONS. BUT KOUMBA TELLS
HIM IT IS NONE OF HIS BUSINESS, THAT SHE IS
OLD ENOUGH TO TAKE CARE OF HERSELF.

CHARLES FINALLY PROPOSES TO MARRY KOUMBA AT THE AGE OF FIFTY, AND KOUMBA ACCEPTS HIS PROPOSAL.

MIRACULOUSLY, KOUMBA IS ABLE TO CONCEIVE AND HAS A BABY FOR CHARLES.

AFTER KOUMBA HAD HER BABY, AARON WAS ASKED TO MOVE OUT. KOUMBA DECIDES TO RENT AN APPARTMENT FOR AARON, SHE OFFERS TO PAY THE RENT. AARON ACCEPTS AND MOVES OUT OF THE HOUSE.

AARON IS STILL HANGING AROUND, SAYING HE IS COMING TO THEIR HOME TO SEE MARTIN.

CHARLES HATES THE IDEA OF HAVING AARON IN THEIR HOME, BUT ACCEPTS IT FOR THE SAKE OF MARTIN.

AARON DOES NOT EVEN HAVE A GIRLFRIEND AND STILL IS DOING EVERYTHING TO GET KOUMBA BACK. NOT BECAUSE HE STILL LOVES HER, BUT JUST TO PROVE TO CHARLES THAT HE CAN HAVE KOUMBA BACK ANYTIME HE WANTS.

BUT KOUMBA REFUSES TO GIVE IN TO AARON'S PLANS. AARON GOES INTO KOUMBA'S OFFICE SEVERAL TIMES DURING THE DAY TO

REMIND HER THAT IT IS THANKS TO HIM THAT SHE IS SOMEBODY TODAY.

KOUMBA REMINDS HIM OFTEN THAT IT WAS BECAUSE OF WHAT HE DID WITH HER "BEST FRIEND" THAT SHE IS THE SOLE OWNER OF KOUMBARON PRODUCTION TODAY.

AARON TELLS KOUMBA THAT HE WILL NEVER GIVE HER UP. BUT KOUMBA KNOWS THAT IT IS NOT TRUE.

SHE KNOWS THAT AARON WANTS KOUM- BARON PRODUCTION BACK, THAT'S ALL, AND THAT HE IS NOT GOING TO STOP AT ANY- THING TO HAVE IT BACK.

AARON NOTICES THAT EVERYTHING HE HAS BEEN DOING TO GET KOUMBA BACK IN HIS ARMS IS NOT WORKING TO HIS ADVANTAGE.

HE ALMOST LOSES HIS JOB AT KOUMBARON ON AN OCCASION. HE TRIES TO WIN THE CUSTODY OF MARTIN, WHO IS NOW FIFTEEN YEARS OLD, BUT STILL LOSES IT TO KOUMBA.

AARON DECIDES TO LEAVE WEST VIRGINIA, ASKING KOUMBA FOR A LOAN OF $200,000.

WHEN KOUMBA LEARNS OF AARON'S PROJECT TO LEAVE WEST VIRGINIA, SHE LOANS HIM THE MONEY.

KNOWING FULLY WELL THAT THERE IS NO WAY HE IS GOING TO PAY HER BACK,

SHE DOES IT TO HAVE PEACE OF MIND AND MAKE CHARLES HAPPY.

KOUMBA AND CHARLES HAVE HAD TO ARGUE MANY TIMES BECAUSE OF AARON. CHARLES OFTEN QUESTIONS KOUMBA'S FIDELITY TO HIM. THE IDEA OF KOUMBA AND AARON WORKING TOGETHER FRIGHTENS CHARLES.

WHEN KOUMBA TELLS CHARLES THAT AARON WANTS A LOAN OF $200,000 TO GET OUT OF TOWN, CHARLES QUICKLY SUPPORTS IT, KNOWING THAT AARON IS GOING TO BE OUT OF THE PICTURE FOR A WHILE AND, IF THEY ARE LUCKY, FOREVER.

AARON GETS THE MONEY, GOES OUT OF TOWN, AND NEVER CALLS BACK TO EVEN SAY THANK YOU OR ASK OF HIS SON.

MARTIN OFTEN ASKS KOUMBA WHERE HIS FATHER IS, BUT KOUMBA DOESN'T HAVE AN ANSWER.

AARON REFUSES TO CONTACT HIS MOTHER AND FATHER. NOBODY KNOWS WHERE HE IS. THIS IS FRIGHTENING FOR KOUMBA, WHO IS AFRAID SOMETHING BAD MUST HAVE HAP-

PENED TO AARON FOR HIM NOT TO HAVE EVEN CONTACTED HIS SON.

WITHOUT TELLING CHARLES, KOUMBA SECRETLY HIRES A PRIVATE DETECTIVE TO LOOK FOR AARON.

AARON IS FOUND SIX MONTHS LATER IN A REHABILITATION CENTER IN GEORGIA.

HE HAD A CAR ACCIDENT SOON AFTER LEAVING WEST VIRGINIA AND HAS SINCE NOT BEEN ABLE TO RECOVER FROM HIS INJURIES.

KOUMBA GOES TO THE REHABILITATION CENTER IN GEORGIA TO SEE AARON.

WHEN KOUMBA GETS THERE, SHE DOESN'T RECOGNIZE AARON. SHE WEEPS BITTERLY AND DECIDES TO HAVE AARON RELEASED TO HER.

KOUMBA TAKES AARON BACK TO A PRIVATE INTENSIVE CARE UNIT IN WEST VIRGINIA. CHARLES IGNORES ALL THESE AND DOES NOT EVEN KNOW THAT KOUMBA HAS FOUND AARON.

KOUMBA SECRETLY GOES TO SEE AARON AT THE CLINIC TWICE A WEEK TILL HE RECOVERS FULLY A YEAR LATER.

WHEN AARON LEARNS THAT KOUMBA CAME TO HIS RESCUE, HE FEELS GUILTY FOR EVERYTHING HE HAS DONE TO HER.

HE ATTEMPTS TO COMMIT SUICIDE, BUT DOES NOT SUCCEED. HE INSTEAD LOSES THE USE OF HIS LEGS AS A RESULT OF THE MEDICATION HE TOOK TO COMMIT SUICIDE.

KOUMBA FEELS GUILTY AND CAN'T JUST LEAVE AARON IN A CLINIC. SHE NOW SPEAKS TO CHARLES ABOUT EVERYTHING SHE HAS DONE TO FIND AARON AND TO CARE FOR HIM IN THE SPECIAL CARE UNIT.

CHARLES IS HURT AND DECIDES TO LEAVE KOUMBA.

KOUMBA NOW RETAINS THE FULL CONTROL OF KOUMBARON PRODUCTION, HAS THE CUSTODY OF HER SON, AND DECIDES SHE IS TOO OLD TO REMARRY. SHE DOES NOT DATE ANYONE ELSE.

SHE BRINGS AARON INTO HER HOME AND LOOKS AFTER HIM TILL HE GIVES UP THE GHOST FIVE YEARS LATER.

KOUMBA GIVES UP THE GHOST IN WEST VIRGINIA TWO YEARS AFTER THE DEATH OF AARON.

SHE HAS WILLED ALL HER FORTUNE TO HER KIDS, WHO STARTED MANAGING KOUM-BARON PRODUCTION YEARS BEFORE HER DEATH.

ON KOUMBA'S DEATHBED, SHE PROCLAIMED, *"I HAVE LIVED A FULFILLED LIFE AND THANK GOD FOR IT. AMERICA IS TRULY THE LAND OF THE FREE AND THE HOME OF THE BRAVE!*

I CAME TO THIS FREE LAND WITH NOTHING, I LIVED IN IT WITH EVERYTHING! I AM LEAV-ING IT NOW. I AM LEAVING EVERY BLESSINGS I RECEIVED OF THIS FREE LAND FOR MY KID. GOD BLESS AMERICA! GOD BLESS AMERICA! GOD BLESS AMERICA!" . AND KOUMBA CLOSES HER EYES, TAKE HER LAST DEEP BREATHE, AND LEAVES THIS WORLD WITH A SMILE ON HER FACE.